Racial and Ethnic
Relations

ELEMENTS OF SOCIOLOGY
A Series of Introductions

Racial and Ethnic Relations

Joseph S. Himes

University of North Carolina,
Greensboro

WM. C. BROWN COMPANY PUBLISHERS
Dubuque, Iowa

Sociology Series

Consulting Editors

Ann Lennarson Greer
University of Wisconsin-Milwaukee

Scott Greer
Northwestern University

Contents

Preface

FOR many people "racial" and "ethnic" are alarm words. They are reminders of Watts and Wounded Knee, of Stokeley Carmichael and Cesar Chavez, of the Black Panther Party and the American Indian Movement. But racial and ethnic also indicate a complex network of relations that lock all the divergent peoples of America into an inclusive social system.

This book is a systematic study of that network of social relations. It asks who the racial and ethnic people are, and what their salient characteristics are. We see the racially and ethnically divergent people of America as members of groups that are called "dominant" and "minority." Considerable space is given to examining the social organizations and cultures, i.e., values and ways, of the racial and ethnic minority groups.

The focus of interest throughout this book is the changing patterns of relations between dominant and minority groups. We note the growth of intergroup conflict and consider the possibility of a viable social policy to govern these relations.

Although many people have contributed to the writing of this book, a few must be singled out for thanks. Mrs. Barbara Comstock Boring, Miss Tanita A. Goodwin, and Mrs. Linda Newman assisted in the research and preparation of the manuscript. My thanks go to Mrs. Betty W. Deskins for typing and retyping, and to my wife, Estelle, for proofreading the manuscript. I also acknowledge with thanks the support and assistance given by the editors, Professor Scott A. Greer and Mr. Robert D. Nash.

Joseph S. Himes

Introduction

THIS book is a brief introduction to the study of racial and ethnic relations. Its main task is to acquaint readers with the basic information, explanations, and literature of the field. With this introduction, those who are interested may proceed with more extensive study. References at the end of each chapter will show the reader where to find fuller treatment of the issues considered.

This book examines some of the major issues in the relation between dominant and minority groups. For the sake of sharpness and clarity, these problems can be stated in the following questions.

How many minority people are there in the United States; what are their salient demographic, social, and economic characteristics?

Where are they located; how well are they integrated within the ecological and social structure of the society?

What (if anything) is distinctive of the social organization and culture of the minority peoples?

Are the racial and ethnic minorities disappearing or changing through the process of cultural assimilation or in the societal "melting pot?"

Are these minorities retaining their separate identities within some pattern of cultural or societal pluralism?

What are the significant trends in intergroup—dominant-minority relations—toward greater cooperation, stable accomodation, or increased struggle?

Is there any American social policy for the racial and ethnic minorities?

What should be the provisions of such a policy and who should take leadership in formulating and implementing it?

Each of these questions is taken up in the chapters that follow. As one reads these pages, he is cautioned that the study of racial and ethnic relations is beset by difficulties that are less troublesome in other areas of sociology. First, members of the dominant and minority groups often have incomplete, inaccurate, or incorrect information about each other. Much of the empirically tested knowledge in this field has not yet become accessible to members of these groups. Lacking accurate information, they seize upon half-truths or outright distortions to meet their need or desire for understanding. Much of what passes for knowledge of these groups is a mixture of myth, fantasy, and gossip. Yet many of us accept this mixture of truth and half-truth because we have no other information.

Second, study and understanding in this field are further hampered by the tendency of each group to evaluate the others and to generate derogatory or hostile feelings based on these evaluations. We often note that the dominants hold the minorities in low esteem because of their racial and cultural characteristics. They also hold feeling-states consistent with these evaluations. In response, the minorities produce reciprocal evaluations and feelings that reveal their interpretation of the intergroup situation. Such evaluations and feelings operate to obstruct objective, judicious examination of the facts of intergroup relations.

Third, each group has produced a set of attitudes and behavior patterns to govern its relations with the others. These clusters of feelings, attitudes, and habits are called prejudices; they function to guide relations between the various groups and to impede objective study and clear understanding.

To caution the reader to be on the alert for these hindrances to the study of intergroup relations is not to say that the scientific study of racial and cultural relations is impossible. Rather such caution is intended to put the reader on guard against these obstacles and to stimulate self-awareness within him. We cannot get rid of our ignorance and prejudices just by wishing; however, we can strive to recognize them, to bring them out into the open, and then to discount or compensate for them. This effort to deal openly and honestly with one's mental and emotional distortions is what we mean by "objectivity."

1 | Dominant and Minority Groups

SOCIOLOGY is the systematic study of social relations.[1] The topic of study may be relations between two or more groups of adolescents, city dwellers, or men in prison. In these examples the social relations are qualified by similarity of the groups. At another time we may investigate relations between groups of adolescents and adults, of city and country people, or of groups of prisoners and prison officials. In these situations social relations are conditioned by the differences of the groups. Another area of considerable sociological study is the relationship between blacks and whites, Jews and gentiles, Puerto-Ricans and mainland North Americans, and so on. In these cases social relations may be strongly affected by differences of racial and cultural characteristics.

DOMINANT and MINORITY GROUPS

The focus of this book is the study of social relations between groups in the United States that differ in racial and/or cultural characteristics. Most Americans are white. They have descended from Anglo-Saxon and other North European ancestors (e.g., German, Scandinavian, Dutch), and have lived in the United States for several generations. Although most of these people are Protestants, a significant and increasing number are Roman Catholics and Jews.[2] Having lived in the United States for a long time, they know and are part of the "American" culture. This large body of Americans (over four-fifths of the total population) is called the dominant group.[3]

Some other Americans are differentiated from the dominant group by physical and/or cultural characteristics. These people include blacks, American Indians, Mexicans, the Orientals, many Puerto Ricans, and a few others who differ in color and other physical characteristics from the dominant white group. Some of these people practice alien religions, for example, Hinduism, and Buddhism, as well as forms of Catholicism and Judaism that differ from those prac-

1. Joseph S. Himes, *The Study of Sociology* (Glenview, Ill.: Scott, Foresman, 1968), p. 2.
2. See Will Herberg, *Protestant-Catholic-Jew* (Garden City: Doubleday, 1955).
3. In this connection see George E. Simpson and J. Milton Yinger, *Racial and Cultural Minorities: An Analysis of Prejudice and Discrimination* (New York: Harper and Row, 1972), pp. 11-13 and Charles F. Marden and Gladys Meyer, *Minorities in American Society* (New York: American Book Co., 1968), pp. 23-24.

ticed by the dominants. These people also practice other forms of culture that differ to one degree or another from that of the whites. This is true of recently arrived Mexicans and Puerto Ricans, of foreign-born Japanese and Chinese, of many blacks, Jews, and Indians. The groups that differ from the dominant group in both racial and cultural characteristics are called racial and/or ethnic minority groups or simply minority groups.

The dominant group controls the higher statuses and prevailing power in the society. This is why the word "dominant" is a better designation for this group than "majority." On the other hand, the racial and ethnic groups are minorities not only because of their comparatively smaller numbers (less than a fifth of the total population), and their physical and cultural characteristics, but also because of their inferiority to the dominants in both status and power. Sociologically, differences of status and power are more important than differences of race and culture.

Before the end of the eighteenth century, the dominants had established their physical and cultural characteristics as the standards for judging outsiders and newcomers. Those who differed in one or both respects were held in low esteem and excluded from acceptance into the dominant group. However, whites and their children who learned the culture of the dominants and accepted their religion might expect to join the dominant group. This practice of evaluating people by reference to characteristics of the dominant group, and of ordering social relations with them on the basis of this evaluation, is called the *norm of color and culture*. All social relations between dominant and minority groups are conditioned by this norm.

THE MINORITY GROUPS

There are many racial and ethnic minority groups in the United States. For example, small colonies of East Indians, French Canadians, Koreans, Arabs, and the like can be found scattered throughout the country. The white European immigrants, such as Swedes, Germans, Poles, and Italians are sometimes called minorities. However, groups like those just mentioned are not discussed specifically in this book for two reasons. First, they are too numerous to be covered in a short volume. Second, and more important is the fact that the first generation white European immigrants are dying out and most of their American-born children and grandchildren—Protestant, Roman Catholic, and Jewish—are being absorbed into the dominant group. Although these groups are not treated specifically in this book, the discussion is generally typical of their situation and social relations. The specific minority groups that are studied in this book include American blacks, Jews, Mexicans, Puerto Ricans, American Indians, Japanese, and Chinese.

These peoples became racial and ethnic minorities in various ways.[4] In every case, when they entered the society, they already possessed physical and cultural traits that distinguished them from the dominant group. Raymond Mack has pointed out that,

4. See Peter I. Rose, *They and We* (New York: Random House, 1964), Chapter 2.
Marden and Meyer, *Minorities in American Society,* Chapters 6 through 18.
Simpson and Yinger, *Racial and Cultural Minorities,* Chapters 9 and 10.

like many other peoples, they entered the society and were assigned minority-group status by some combination of colonialism, annexation, voluntary migration, or involuntary migration.[5] Thus many Spanish-speaking and Mexican people became an American minority group when Arizona and New Mexico were annexed in 1848 following the Mexican War. The Puerto Ricans, Japanese, and Chinese migrated voluntarily, but the ancestors of the present blacks were brought against their will. The American Indians were subjugated, herded into reservations, and reduced to minority status by white settlers and the national government.

A FRAME OF REFERENCE FOR STUDYING INTERGROUP RELATIONS

A group's life chances and experiences are conditioned by the nature of the social system within which it lives, as well as by that group's ability to meet the needs of that social system and to fulfill the societal expectations. The American social system is said to be democratic with an open class pattern that encourages groups and individuals to strive for advancement and advantage on the basis of "merit." However, many conditions affect the operation of the societal and class systems. In the American system, the norm of color and culture differentially conditions the life chances and experiences of dominants and minorities. The critical factors are arranged in such a way as to give the dominants the advantage and to set special obstacles for the minorities.

Mere participation of these groups within the social system requires basic cooperation which has been patterned as acculturation, accomodation, and assimilation. These interactive patterns both accept and facilitate the unequal positions and situations of dominant and minority groups. Many observers focus on these patterns and tend to maximize the process of cooperation in their analyses of intergroup relations.

Although intergroup relations can be viewed in varying patterns of cooperation, it may be more accurate to say that such relations are mainly conflict relations. This fact issues from the efforts of the dominant white group to enforce or enhance the social status quo and the responding efforts of the minorities to alter or circumvent it. The minority response to this inequitable structure and situation can be described in three ways. First, while resenting the system that invites them to compete and achieve but denies them equal opportunity, some individuals seek to accommodate by making the best adjustment they can. Second, some others, resenting the system no less, and for the same reasons, may nevertheless seek rather to manipulate it, extracting from it whatever advantage they can. And third, an increasing number of minority people also resenting the system for the same reasons, may attack it (and the dominants who control and profit from it) in varying patterns of overt struggle. The study of dominant-minority relations must recognize this mixture of relationship patterns and the trend of relations toward increasing intergroup struggle.

Summary

In this chapter, then, dominant and minority groups are differentiated and de-

5. See Raymond W. Mack, *Race, Class and Power* (New York: American Book Co., 1968) p. 227.

fined, the processes of forming minorities are mentioned, and the seven leading racial and ethnic minorities are named. The norm of color and culture is said to be the central force governing intergroup relations. Readers are cautioned against prejudice as a serious hindrance in the study of these relations. The chapter ends with a frame of reference in which it is shown that status and power tend to emphasize struggle rather than cooperation as the major interactive pattern.

For Further Reading

Baxter, Paul and Sanson, Basil. *Race and Social Difference*, Baltimore: Penguin Books, 1972.

Viewing race as a social rather than biological fact, the authors show how sterotypes and prejudices emerge.

Cohen, Robert. *The Color of Man*, New York: Bantam Books, 1972.

Facts about human color and how it is transmitted from one generation to the next.

Mack, Raymond W. *Race, Class, and Power*, New York: Van Nostrand Reinhold Company, 1968, Chapters 1 through 6.

Relations between dominant and minority groups are stated in terms of social class and social power.

Marden, Charles F. and Meyer, Gladys. *Minorities in American Society*, New York: Van Nostrand Reinhold Company, 1968, Chapters 1 through 5.

These authors employ a sociological approach in the study of racial and ethnic relations in the United States.

Martin, James G. and Franklin, Clyde W. *Minority Group Relations*, Columbus: Merrill Publishing Company, 1973, Chapters 1 through 4.

This book establishes a social-psychological approach to the study of intergroup relations.

Rose, Peter I. *They and We*, New York: Random House, 1964.

A short paperback text on intergroup relations in the United States.

Simpson, George E. and Yinger, J. Milton. *Racial and Cultural Minorities*, New York: Harper and Row ,1972, Chapters 1 through 8.

A well known statement of the social-psychological approach.

Stalvey, Lois Mark. *The Education of WASP*, New York: Bantam Books, 1971.

A typical middle-class white Anglo-Saxon family discover racism.

2 | The Minority People

IN this chapter we ask: Who are the minority peoples? What are their salient characteristics? We answer by presenting some data that describe their demographic, ecological and socioeconomic characteristics. With this information in hand, we can proceed in the following chapters to study the patterns of interaction between these minorities and the dominant group.

DEMOGRAPHIC CHARACTERISTICS

Size

Table 1 shows the size of each minority group and indicates the percentage it constitutes of the total United States population. It is seen that blacks, as the largest minority group, outnumber all the others together. Numerically, only the blacks at 11.1 percent constitute a significant part of the total population. Jews and Mexicans, the next largest groups, are only about one-fourth as numerous as blacks. American Indians, Japanese, and Chinese are the smallest minorities included in this table.[1] In the aggregate, the seven minorities included in this table total some thirty-seven million persons and comprise nearly one-fifth of the total population of the United

TABLE 1

POPULATIONS OF THE SEVEN MINORITIES BY NUMBERS AND BY PERCENT OF TOTAL UNITED STATES POPULATION[1]

Group	Number	Percent of Total
Total Population	204,800,000	100.0
American blacks	22,580,289	11.1
Jews	5,878,555 (1968)[2]	2.9
Mexicans	5,254,000 (1972)	2.6
Puerto Ricans	1,518,000 (1972)	0.7
American Indians	792,730[3]	0.4
Japanese	591,290	0.3
Chinese	435,062	0.2

1. As of this writing, publications of the 1970 census of population include incomplete figures for the racial and ethnic minorities. Blacks and Spanish-speaking people are most fully reported. Except as specifically noted, the figures included in this table and throughout this chapter have been taken from reports of the 1970 census of population, various numbers of the Current Population Reports, and other sample surveys conducted by the Bureau of the Census. Parenthetical dates indicate that the figures are derived from sample surveys. Because of the great number and diversity of sources, census figures are not footnoted individually.

2. *Encyclopedia Judaica*, (Jerusalem: 1971) pp. 1,647-48.

3. Residing in continental United States. In 1970, an additional 50,270 Eskimos and Aleuts resided in Alaska and were included in the total Indian population.

1. In 1970 the Bureau of the Census enumerated 343,060 Filipinos in the United States. In addition, there were many other even smaller ethnic and racial minority groups.

5

States. Thus, numerically speaking, the racial and ethnic minorities are important.

These minority populations continue to grow by both immigration and by natural increase. Puerto Ricans still come to the mainland, although the rate of migration has slowed down. Between 1967 and 1970, 178,319 Mexicans, 73,095 Chinese (from Taiwan and Hong Kong) and 16,761 Japanese immigrants entered the United States.[2]

All these minorities continue to grow by natural increase, that is, rate of birth is higher than rate of death. Natural increase is the major source of growth of the black and Indian populations. Between 1960 and 1970, blacks increased by 19.7 percent while the Indians more than doubled, increasing by 51.2 percent. With the exception of the Jews, all these minorities reveal birth rates exceeding that of whites. In 1971, for women 35 to 44 years old, respective birth rates were: white 2.9; blacks 3.6; Jews 1.7; Mexicans 4.4; Puerto Ricans 3.6; and American Indians 7.3.[3]

In 1960, the Bureau of the Census reported that only 9,738,000 persons born outside the United States were residing within the country, in spite of the fact that over 50 million had come during the 150 years that records have been kept. The American-born children of these immigrants, both living and dead, are both legally and culturally American. The native-born children of white immigrants tend to move, through assimilation, into the dominant group. Most of the foreign-born individuals, all non-whites, whether foreign-born or native-born, and some native-born children of white immigrants are still excluded from membership in the dominant group, and they must be understood as occupying some kind of minority-group status.

There are now close to fifty million Roman Catholics in the United States. The white-native-born, culturally assimilated Roman Catholics have tended to enter the dominant group. Non-whites from Mexico and Puerto Rico, first-generation immigrants from Europe and the Americas and a few other Catholics are still found in the ranks of the minority groups. Thus, several million individuals other than those listed in Table 1 also occupy minority status by reason of their alien culture and race.

Sex

There are fewer men than women in the United States population. This fact is revealed by a sex ratio (number of men per 100 women) of 94.8 as shown in the left hand column of Table 2. Only blacks at 90.8

TABLE 2

SEX RATIOS AND MEDIAN AGES OF THE UNITED STATES POPULATION AND THE SEVEN MINORITY GROUPS

Group	Sex Ratio	Median Age
U. S. Population	94.8	28.3
Blacks	90.8	21.4
Jews	96.5 (1968)	36.2[1]
Mexicans	97.4 (1969)	18.6 (1972)
Puerto Ricans	96.2 (1969)	17.9
American Indians	97.3 (1969)	...
Japanese	117.9	28.8[2]
Chinese	90.0	27.4

1. Sidney Goldstein and Calvin Goldschneider, *Jewish Americans* (Englewood Cliffs: Prentice-Hall, 1968), pp. 44-45.

2. For median ages of Japanese and Chinese see Harry H. L. Kitano, *Japanese Americans: Evolution of a Subculture* (Englewood Cliffs: Prentice-Hall 1969), pp. 168-69.

2. *Statistical Abstract of the United States 1971*, Table 135, p. 92.

3. *Current Population Reports, Population Characteristics*, "Fertility Variations by Ethnic Origin," Series P 20, No. 226, November, 1971, p. 1.

and Chinese at 90.0 reveal sex ratios below that of the total population. A low sex ratio in the black population has been reported for many years.[4] The paucity of men in relation to women among the Chinese is related to their social experiences in the United States.

All the other minorities reveal sex ratios higher than that of the total United States population. However, only the Japanese are really outstanding in this respect. The Japanese sex ratio of 117.9 is one of the highest in the country. This high sex ratio is a consequence of the migration that brought the early Japanese population to the United States.[5] Virtually all the first Japanese immigrants were men, and although women came later, they still remain outnumbered.

Such "abnormal" sex ratios are likely to have some effects upon intergroup relations. For example, the paucity of men among the blacks and Chinese and the excess of men in the Japanese group are reflected in composition of the respective work forces, conditions of marriage and family life, and various aspects of community organization and educational experience.

Age

Median ages (the ages that divide populations into older and younger halves) are shown in the right-hand column of Table 2. It is seen that Jews at 36.2, Japanese at 28.8 and Chinese at 27.4 exceed or approximate the median of 28.3 of the total population. Blacks, Mexicans, Puerto Ricans and Indians are younger, sometimes strikingly younger, than the whites.

The social implications of age differentials are revealed more clearly in age composition data. The percentages of minority persons under age 18; blacks 48.0; Mexicans 48.6; and Puerto Ricans 50.2, exceed the 35.5 percentage of whites in this age category. In 1968, the Jews reported 26.0 percent of their ethnic group under 16 years of age.[6] On the other hand, blacks, Mexicans, and Puerto Ricans showed fewer persons 65 years old and older than all Americans; the percentages being 6.2, 3.2, and 2.0 respectively, as compared with 9.9 for the general population. At the same time, the proportion of these three groups in the 18-64 age period is below that of the total population. In 1970, 55.9 percent of the total fell in this age period, but only 49.2 percent of blacks, 48.2 percent of Mexicans, and 47.8 percent of Puerto Ricans were between 18 and 64 years of age.

Figures were not available for Japanese, Chinese, and Indians. However, we can speculate that the Japanese and Chinese populations may resemble the general American population in their age compositions. The Indians, however, with a very high birth rate and high death rate will reveal a higher percentage under 18 and a lower percentage over 65 years of age.

With ratification of the Twenty-Sixth Constitutional Amendment(1971) and subsequent adjustive legislation, social adulthood has been moved from age 21 to 18. Persons under this age comprise the youthful dependency group which is shown to be very large in the black, Mexican, Puerto Rican, and Indian groups, and abnormally

4. E. Franklin Frazier, *The Negro in the United States* (New York: Macmillan, 1957), pp. 180-82.
5. Marden and Meyer, *Minorities in American Society*, p. 199.
6. Goldstein and Goldschneider, *Jewish Americans*, pp. 41-42.

small among the Jews. On the other hand, the old-age dependency groups are relatively small among blacks, Mexicans, Puerto Ricans, and Indians, and about average in the Jewish group. The broad age bracket— 18 to 64 years—covers the work force which is large in the general population and Jewish group, but constricted in the other minorities. These variable age characteristics are associated with differential socioeconomic conditions of the minorities which will be examined later.

ECOLOGICAL CHARACTERISTICS

In the folklore of racial and ethnic relations certain groups are associated with certain regions or locations. Thus, blacks are thought to belong in the rural South, Jews in big eastern cities, and Orientals on the West Coast. Identification of the minorities with ecological locales is related to their history in the society and the points of their entry as immigrants.

Regional Distribution

Two-thirds and more of the Jews and Puerto Ricans are concentrated in the Northeast.[7] Just over a quarter of the Chinese, 26.5 percent, and just under a fifth of the blacks, 19.0 percent, reside in this region. Over half of the blacks, 53 percent are in the South, although they are no longer concentrated in agriculture. Nearly three-quarters of the Mexican population is concentrated in the five southwestern states of California, New Mexico, Arizona, Texas, and Colorado.

The Japanese and Chinese are concentrated in the West. Fewer than a fifth of the Japanese, 18 percent, live outside the western region. Even after the traumatic World

War II experience of being forcibly uprooted and confined in Relocation Centers, 82 percent of the Japanese reside in the West. The legends of Chinatowns in San Francisco and other west coast cities would lead one to expect that more than the reported 55.6 percent of the Chinese live in the West. Over a quarter of the Chinese 26.5 percent, live in the Northeast.

Almost three-fifths, 58 percent, of the Indians live on reservations in the 48 states and Alaska. Indian territories have shrunk from the total land area of the United States to some 55 million acres.[8] Although a quarter of the Indians, 25.4 percent, live in the South, almost half, 49.3 percent, reside in the West. The North Central region contains fewer minority people than any; Indians with 19.1 and blacks with 20 percent being the most numerous.

These profiles of regional distribution are of interest to our study since the so-called "problems" of intergroup relations tend to be identified with the locales of minority-group concentration. Thus the "Negro problem" has historically been thought of as a phenomenon of southern life, although recently it has spread to other regions. Anti-Semitism is most typical of the populous Northeast. Relations with Mexicans, Japanese, and Chinese have developed as problematical mainly in the West and

7. The Bureau of the Census groups the states into four major geographic regions. The Northeast includes 9 states known as New England and the Mid Atlantic area. The North Central includes 12 states from Ohio to Minnesota and the Dakotas. The South has 16 states stretching from Delaware and Flordia on the east to Texas on the west. The West includes 11 states designated as Mountain and Pacific.

8. Alvin M. Josephy, Jr., "Wounded Knee and All That," *New York Times Magazine*, March 18, 1973, p. 19.

Southwest. In every case geography is influenced by history, and both tend to condition the web of intergroup relations. In every case also, the tradition and fabric of intergroup relations are unique to some degree.

Urban-Rural Distribution

The urban-rural distinction is as significant as region in the understanding of dominant-minority relations. Including only non reservation Indians, the minority groups are typically urban people. It makes little difference whether they reside in northern, southern, or western cities, they live under modern urban conditions. Perhaps even more significant is the fact that while the United States population has been becoming steadily more urban, the minority groups have been urbanizing at an even faster pace. From this perspective we must say that dominant-minority relations are urban relations with the implications of heterogeneity, competition, and impersonality which that fact suggests.

Over nine-tenths of the Chinese, Jews, and Puerto Ricans, 96.3, 96.1 and 91.0 percents respectively, live in cities, mainly large eastern cities. Four-fifths, 81.4 percent, of the blacks are urban dwellers. This is true in spite of the fact mentioned earlier that 53 percent of these people still reside in the South. Despite a popular stereotype of the migratory Mexican farm worker, most Mexicans are city dwellers. The Japanese are nearly nine-tenths urban, 88.7 percent.

Urban Centralization

The minority groups are not only typically urban, they are also sharply centralized in the older, deteriorated sections of big cities. Concentration in central cities of metropolitan areas is influenced by both the norm of color and culture and by rapid suburbanization of big city whites. This trend of the minority-group populations continues, both from migration and especially from net increase of the urban sectors.

Half or more of the urban black, Puerto Rican, Mexican, and Chinese populations reside in central cities of big metropolitan areas. Just under half of the Japanese, 48.2 percent, also occupy central city locations.

Concentration of these minority peoples in the deteriorated sections of big cities contributes to the formation of ghetto-like communities. "The formation of black ghettos resulted from the reciprocal operation of several socioeconomic processes."[9] People are located in the oldest and most deteriorated sections. Complex legal, *de facto*, and voluntary segregation accentuates population congestion.[10] Public facilities (schools, hospitals, welfare services, police and fire protection), cultural facilities, streets, and rubbish collection, tend to be among the worst in the cities. Segregation also functions to limit the access of ghetto dwellers to facilities and opportunities outside the ghetto. These conditions set the stage for the "cycle of poverty" which is the typical lot of many ghetto dwellers. These areas tend to be both deviantly organized and chronically disorganized.

Central-city minority populations increase by both migration and reproduction.

9. Joseph S. Himes, *Racial Conflict in American Society* (Columbus: Merrill, 1973), pp. 129-130.
10. Amos H. Hawley and Vincent P. Rock, eds., *Segregation in Residential Areas* (Washington: National Academy of Sciences, 1973).

However, growth by migration is declining. As noted above, some Mexicans, Puerto Ricans, and Orientals still enter the United States as immigrants. Migration from rural to urban locations is slowing down.

Growth of the minority urban populations results mainly from net increase, i.e., excess of births over deaths. This fact is suggested by the high birth rates and low median ages presented in an earlier section of this chapter. In the half decade from 1960 to 1964, 55.9 percent of new central-city blacks were urban-born, while during the second five years, 1964-69, 71 percent were central-city natives.[11] This fact is further confirmed in the case of central-city blacks by a 1969 census report.

Most of the estimated 2.6 million increase since 1960 in the Negro population in central cities is due to the natural increase of the population. . . . About one-third of the net gain— approximately 800,000 persons—is due to net in-migration. The decline in the white population of central cities, on the other hand, implies a substantial net out-migration of the white population during this period.[12]

The Jewish population is concentrated in suburban places surrounding large eastern cities. In all geographic regions very few Jews are found residing in locations outside the suburbs. Over a quarter of the Japanese, 27.4 percent, and more than a fifth of the Chinese, 21.2 percent, are also located in the suburban fringes of metropolitan areas. Suburban dwellers among the others minorities comprise around a tenth or less of their populations.

At present about forty-two percent of the Indian population reside off federal and state reservations. Not all of these, however, are city-dwellers. Urban-dwelling Indians, like the other poor minority groups, are huddled in ghetto-like communities of central cities. Only negligible proportions of Indians have found their way to the suburbs.

SOCIOECONOMIC CHARACTERISTICS

A considerable folklore has developed around the economic situation of the minorities. For example, it is widely believed that all Jews are rich and that their wealth is attributable to a special kind of "racial" business acumen. On the other hand, blacks are known to be poor. In some quarters their poverty is explained by a "racial" bent toward improvidence and extravagance. The Japanese, who are often imagined to be well-off, are said to be crafty and ruthless in economic dealings. These stereotypes tend to influence intergroup relations and therefore, must be taken into account in our study. This section of the chapter will describe the socioeconomic conditions of the several minorities by examining some facts of education, occupation, income, and poverty experience.

Education

To indicate the educational situation we use average years of schooling completed by persons 25-years-old and over. Census data report that in the American population 25-years-old and older, the average educational achievement is 12.1. That is, on an average, Americans have finished high school. Recent data indicate that Jews, 12.8,

11. Joseph S. Himes, "Some Characteristics of the Migration of Blacks in the United States," *Social Biology*, 18:363, (December, 1971).

12. *Current Population Reports*, "The Social and Economic Status of Negroes in the United States," Series P 23, No. 29, 1969, p. ix.

and Japanese, 12.2, exceed this average.[13] These figures are not surprising, for both the Jews and Japanese have demonstrated a group concern for education. The Chinese with average years of schooling of 11.1 are not far below the national average, but above other minority groups.

All the other minorities are significantly below the national average in years of schooling. The respective figures are blacks 10.8, Mexicans 10.8, Puerto Ricans 9.9 and Indians 8.4. These data gain their major social significance in respect to employment, occupation and income, although they are also associated with general social experience.

Other educational data confirm these differentials. In 1970, 37.7 percent of blacks but only 23.7 percent of Puerto Ricans had finished high school. In 1970 6.1 percent of blacks had graduated from college. However, Goldstein and Goldschneider reported in 1968 that 22 percent of Jewish family heads were college graduates.[14] Three-fifths, 61.8 percent of blacks and 90.3 percent of Indian children 5 to 18 years of age were in public schools. However, a tenth of Indian children 14 years old and older had no schooling at all and 60 percent had less than an eighth grade education. Virtually all, 99 percent, of Jewish children age 14 to 19 who had not yet graduated from high school were still enrolled in school in 1968.[15]

Occupations

As might be expected, occupational profiles of the minority groups reflect the educational differentials just discussed. In 1970, half the white males were engaged in white-collar occupations. *The American Jewish Yearbook*, referring to the 1957 Census study, reported that almost all gainfully employed Jews, 97 percent, were found in these occupations.[16] Although recent figures were not available, it seems evident that Japanese and Chinese workers were also heavily represented in the white-collar professional managerial, and proprietary occupations. The proportion of blacks, Mexicans, Puerto Ricans, and non-reservation Indians in white-collar occupations was lower. The respective percentages were 20.1, 17.5, 21.5 and 21.7.

Virtually no Jews, 1.9 percent of the Puerto Ricans, and 0.2 percent of non-reservation Indians were engaged in agriculture. No figures were available for Japanese and Chinese. However, the percentage of these groups in farming was also low since these minorities are predominantly urban. Fewer than a twentieth, 4.5 percent of the blacks, and a twelfth of the Mexicans, 8.3 percent, were engaged in farming.

In 1970 just over a third, 34.5 percent, of American whites worked at blue-collar jobs, i. e., skilled and semiskilled. Only negligible percentages of Jewish, Japanese, and Chinese workers were found in these occupations. On the other hand, three fifths and more of the other minorities were confined to these types of jobs. The respective percentages were; blacks 63.7, Mexicans 62.4, Puerto Ricans 59.1, and non-reservation Indians 71.5.

13. Based on findings of the "Providence Study" as quoted by Goldstein and Goldschneider, *Jewish Americans*, p. 67. And Median years of schooling for Japanese and Chinese from William Peterson, *Makers of America: Emergent Minorities 1955-1970*, (New York: Random House, 1971) p. 132.

14. Goldstein and Goldschneider, *Jewish Americans*, p. 66.

15. *Ibid.*, p. 66

16. *American Jewish Yearbook*, Vol. 72, 1972, p. 76.

The 11.7 percent of blacks and Mexicans in service occupations is only slightly larger than the 10.7 percent of whites. However, Puerto Ricans with 17.5 percent have more, and non-reservation Indians with 6.7 percent have fewer persons in these occupations. Because of their involvement in the white-collar services, Jews, Japanese, and Chinese may be proportionately more numerous than whites in these fields. Around three-quarters of the gainfully employed blacks, Mexicans, Puerto Ricans, and non-reservation Indians work at blue-collar and service jobs, but fewer than half, 45.2 percent, of the whites are found in these fields.

The impact of education upon occupation is revealed in the contrast among minorities with reference to white-collar vs. blue-collar and service occupations. The better educated groups, Jews, Japanese, and Chinese reveal substantial proportions of white-collar workers. However, the minorities with limited educational achievements, blacks, Mexicans, Puerto Ricans, and non-reservation Indians, are concentrated in the blue-collar and service jobs. In the case of these latter groups, educational deficiency is augmented by restrictions of the norm of color and culture.[17]

Employment Status

A further economic indicator of the minority groups is their employment status. In 1971, the Bureau of the Census reported the unemployment rate for whites as 5.4 percent of all persons in the labor force. Although exact figures were not available, it seems likely that unemployment among Jews and Japanese did not diverge far from this figure. The other minorities, however, revealed much higher rates of unemployment.

Total unemployment for blacks in 1971 was 9.9 percent, almost double that for whites. In 1972, 3.2 percent of Mexican workers were jobless. However, between ages 16 and 64, male unemployment was 7.9 and female 9.1. Total unemployment among Puerto Ricans in 1972 was 6.5 percent. However, for male and female workers 16 to 64 years old in the work force, the respective rates were 8.8 and 17.6 percent.

Age-linked unemployment rates provide better indicators of economic situation. In 1972, 7.1 percent of Mexican and 5.0 percent of Puerto Rican men 25 to 44 years of age were unemployed. These figures compare favorably with the figure of 5.4 percent unemployment among white American men. However, at the same time, 15.3 percent of Mexican and 25.4 percent of Puerto Rican men 16 to 24 years of age were jobless.

Income and Poverty Experience

The residual effects of educational deficiency, occupational restriction, and unemployment are concentrated in individual and family incomes. In 1969, the median income of white families was $10,083. In 1962 (latest figure available), the median family income of Jews was $9,938, and by the present it has doubtlessly equalled or exceeded that for whites.[18] Median family incomes for all the other minorities fell below those for whites and Jews. Some comparable median family incomes were: blacks $6,280

17. See Joseph S. Himes, "Some Work-Related Cultural Deprivations of Lower-Class Negro Youths," *Journal of Marriage and The Family,* 26:447-449, (November, 1964).

18. Glen Gockel, "Income and Religious Affiliation, "*American Journal of Sociology,* 74:632, (1969).

in 1971; Mexicans $7,486 in 1972; Puerto Ricans $6,185 in 1972; and non-reservation Indians $6,000 estimated in 1971.

In 1969 the "low income" figure separating the poverty from the non-poverty category of individuals was $1,834.[19] Low-income figures were not available for Jews and Japanese, but it seems likely that neither of these groups has had a significant poverty experience. The percentages of individuals falling below this low-income figure were blacks 33.7 in 1970; Mexicans 28.9 in 1972; Puerto Ricans 32.2 in 1972; and non-reservation Indians 45.1, estimated in 1971.

Summary

In summary fashion the minorities can be described in the following way. The seven major minorities in the United States total some 37 million people, just under a fifth of the total. More than half are black and over an eighth each are Jewish and Mexican. Females outnumber males in six of the seven groups. There are almost 12 males for each ten Japanese females, but only 9 males for each ten black or Chinese females.

The Jews, Japanese, and Chinese tended to resemble the white population in age composition. All the other minorities, however, were younger as revealed by median ages, proportion of individuals under 18 years of age, and crude birth rates. These demographic characteristics of sex and age tend to be correlated with some social characteristics of the minority groups.

The minority groups are urban dewllers. From over three-fifths to more than nine-tenths of them reside in cities. Typically, the Jews are suburbanites, and the Japanese and Chinese are moving to the suburbs. Members of the other minorities are concentrated in the central cities of metropolitan areas. Over half the Indians still reside on reservations. In every case, the minorities are moving, though at different rates, into suburban districts of big cities.

Educational achievements of Jews and Japanese either equal or exceed that of the total population. To one degree or another, educational attainments of the other minorities fall short of that reached by all Americans. Variable educational accomplishments of the seven minorities are associated with their economic circumstances. That is, in terms of occupation, income, employment status, and poverty experience, the Jews and Japanese conform to the average American pattern. The other groups tend to diverge from this average in one respect or another. They reveal concentrations in the low-prestige, low-paid occupations, high unemployment rates, low average family and per-capita incomes, and extensive poverty experience.

For Further Reading

Frazier, E. Franklin. *The Negro in the United States,* New York: Macmillan 1957.

A comprehensive sociological study of blacks in the United States.

Goldstein, Sidney and Goldschneider, Calvin. *Jewish Americans,* Englewood Cliffs: Prentice-Hall, 1968.

A competent survey of the Jewish group in the United States.

Heller, Celia Stopnicka. *Mexican American Youth,* New York: Random House, 1966.

A study of the situation of Mexican youth in the Southwest states.

19. See Bureau of the Census, *Social and Economic Characteristics of the Population, North Carolina,* 1970, Appendix 30, Table A.

Josephy, Alvin M. Jr. *The Indian Heritage of America,* New York: Knopf, 1968.

A comprehensive and authoritative book on the Indians.

Hum Lee, Rose. *The Chinese in the United States of America,* Hong Kong: Hong Kong University Press, 1960.

A comprehensive report on the Chinese people in the United States.

Padilla, Elena. *Up From Puerto Rico,* New York: Columbia University Press, 1958.

A graphic account of the Puerto Rican people in New York City.

Peterson, William. *Japanese Americans,* New York: Random House, 1971.

A recent and authoritative study of the Japanese minority in the U.S.

Wheeler, Thomas C. ed., *The Immigrant Experience,* Baltimore: Penguin, 1972.

Original essays on the experience of immigrants to the United States.

3 | Social Organization of the Minorities

POPULAR conceptions of the minorities are sometimes associated with images of their religious organizations. For example, there is the Jewish synagogue, the black Baptist church, the Oriental Buddhist temple, and the Spanish language Mexican Roman Catholic parish. But the organizational portraits of these minorities are equally captured in such words as tribe, tong, or barrio. In spite of these colorful symbols, each minority reveals a system of groups, associations, communities, and institutions that implement its way of life.

In this chapter we will examine the social organizations of the minority groups. The aim is to identify and describe those broad patterns of collective activity and intergroup relations that typify and differentiate life within and among these groups. First, we will see how the minorities are fitted and ordered within the inclusive American social structure. This inquiry should provide a perspective for considering relations between the minorities and the dominant group. Later in this chapter we will examine the forms and patterns of social organization within the several minorities.

MINORITIES IN AMERICAN SOCIAL STRUCTURE

In order to locate the minorities in American social structure it will be necessary to review several kinds of data. First are the facts of residence that place them within the ecological structure. Second, educational, occupational, and income data will permit us to see the place of the minorities within the American social-class system. Third, we will explore the position of the minorities in American social structure from the point of view of their religious affiliations. A fourth clue to the position of the minorities in the inclusive societal organization can be gained from examining their place in large-scale associations and organizations. And finally, we will examine evidence of alienation of the minorities from American society.

Minorities in the Ecological Structure

In the preceding chapter it was shown that although minority people are found in all regions, certain groups tend to be identified with specific regions. Thus, typically Jews and Puerto Ricans live in the Northeast while the Chinese and Japanese are located on the West Coast. Mexicans are identified with the Southwest, Texas to Southern California. The black population is still predominantly eastern, both southern and northern; and the Indians, both reservation and non-reservation, are concentrated in the West.

Most minority people are city dwellers. It is significant in this connection that only two of the minorities, blacks with 4.5 percent and non-reservation Indians with 8.1 percent, exceed the 4 percent of the general population classified as rural. The evidence indicates that most minority people live within the central cities of large metropolitan areas. From one-half to four-fifths of these groups (excluding Jews and Indians) are concentrated in the inner sections of the metropolitan areas. The Indians are still largely restricted to reservations. The Jews are concentrated in suburban communities. A small and increasing percentage of the other minorities—blacks, Mexicans, Orientals and Puerto Ricans—are entering the middle classes and joining the move to the suburbs. This heavy concentration of minority peoples in the old central sections of metropolitan areas provides one clue to their position in American social structure.

Minorities in the Class Structure

It was shown in the preceding chapter that, except for the Jews and Japanese, all the minorities have fewer median years of schooling than the white population. The differential is even greater in amount of higher education. The Jews and Japanese resemble the white population in median years of schooling. More than this, young, American-born members of these minorities

have an outstanding record in higher education. The Chinese, Puerto Ricans, blacks and Mexicans are increasing their median years of schooling and amount of higher education. Yet these minorities remain below national averages in both respects.

Limited education helps to restrict these minority workers to service, blue-collar, and low-prestige white-collar occupations. It was noted that fewer than ten percent of blacks and Mexicans are engaged in agricultural occupations. On the other hand, the well educated, native-born Jews and Japanese are engaged in white-collar professional, technical and managerial activities. Although the other minorities are increasing their educational attainments, they tend to advance in occupational standing at a slower rate. These minority workers find themselves locked into lower-class occupations, not only by limited education, but also by the force of the norm of color and culture.

Limited education and occupational disadvantage work to ensure low incomes for the minority peoples. The data presented in the preceding chapter show that in terms of median annual family income and relationship to the low-income figure, all the minorities fell below the general American population. These differentials were extreme in the case of Indians, Mexicans, blacks and Puerto Ricans, but typically, less in the case of Jews and Orientals.

These data indicate that, with only a few exceptions, the racial and ethnic minorities belong in the lower and working classes. The exception to this generalization is most notable among young, native-born Jews and Japanese, and to a lesser (although increasing) degree among the other minorities. This picture of class placement on the basis of education, occupation, and income corresponds to the ecological concentration of the minorities within the old central sections of large metropolitan areas.

Minorities in the Religious Structure

The dominant religious norm in the United States is still Protestantism. However, as Will Herberg has argued, Catholicism and Judaism have both been Americanized to a significant extent and now form part of the inclusive religious organization.[1] The place of the minorities in American social structure can be revealed in part by considering their religious affiliations in relation to this enlarged religious norm.

Except for a small, though growing minority, blacks are Protestants. Yet, religiously speaking, blacks are regarded as inferior and collateral in the religious structure. Two circumstances account for this fact.

First, most blacks belong to Protestant denominations and congregations that are segregated on the basis of color. Segregated religious organizations among blacks, for which there is no parallel white structure, include Baptists, Colored and African Methodist Episcopal, and African Methodist Episcopal Zion connections, as well as an aggregation of fundamentalist sects. Many other blacks belong to congregations of the Presbyterian, Protestant Episcopal, Methodist, and Christian-Congregational denominations that are, in fact, racially segregated. By the judgment of the norm of color, such denominations and congregations are inferior and collateral in the American religious structure.

Officially, at the legal level, most of the major American Protestant denominations have "desegregated." For many blacks this means only that their all-black or almost all-black congregations are affiliated to bureaucratically desegregated organizations. A growing number of blacks are members of white congregations and so are more or less taken into the religious mainstream.

Second, to one degree or another, the religious practices of blacks deviate from the norm established by the middle-class white Protestant churches. This deviation is dramatic in many of the fundamentalist churches of lower-class blacks. It is less evident in the congregations of middle-class blacks. In every instance though, the religiously dominant whites perceive deviance. Inferiority is revealed in the avoidance and disparaging behavior of the dominant white Protestants who control and regulate the norm.

Most members of the other minorities are non-Protestant and so to some degree deviate from the strict religious norm. But as mentioned above, Roman Catholicism and Judaism have tended to become Americanized. That is, certain forms and manifestations of these religions have conformed, more or less, to the dominant norm. Therefore the communicants of these Americanized Roman Catholic and Jewish congregations tend to conform to the enlarged and inclusive religious norm.

On the other hand, conservative and recent-migrant members of some parishes and synagogues still practice forms of Catholicism and Judaism that are significantly deviant. Thus they tend to draw upon themselves the ethnocentric judgment of deviance and inferiority. Individuals that fall within this category include recent Mexican, Puerto Rican, Chinese, or Jewish immigrants, and individuals who adhere to

1. Will Herberg, *Protestant-Catholic-Jew.*

orthodox practices, for example the Hasidic Jews.

The traditional religions of the Chinese and Japanese exclude them from the dominant American religious community. However, increasing numbers of American-born and well-educated members of these minorities tend to become Protestants. Most American Indians remain far outside the religious pale by reason of their adherence to the various tribal religious systems.

Minorities in Formal Organization

The positions of the minorities in American social structure can also be revealed by examining their participation in formal organizations. This evidence constitutes a clue of structural position since the large formal organizations are the major vehicles of general social life. For this investigation, four types of formal organizations are considered: political parties, labor unions, veterans associations, and civic organizations.

Like most Americans, minority voters belong to the two major political parties, Democratic and Republican. The bulk of minority people are lower-and working-class, and in recent years they have tended to be affiliated with the Democratic Party. As a consequence, since the early thirties when Franklin D. Roosevelt put together the modern Democratic coalition, minorities have participated in the mainstream of government and power. However, their influence has been limited.

Blacks have been prominent in the Democratic Party coalition from the beginning. Steadily, and especially after 1960, the number of blacks registered and voting increased. In the late '60s and early '70s they organized congressional, regional, and national caucuses to try to increase their influence on the national party and governmental processes.

In the 1972 election increasing numbers of black voters switched to the Republican Party. It seems likely that the number of persons registered and voting, the number of black candidates running for and being elected to public office, and the organized efforts of blacks to influence party and governmental operations will increase.[2] At the same time black voters may become more evenly divided between the two major parties than at any time since the Depression.

Jews as predominantly middle-class citizens would seem to be oriented toward the Republican Party. However, their political orientation is also influenced by their minority-group status and by their liberal tradition. Jews, therefore, have participated in both national parties. Because of their liberal tradition they have also been found in the ranks of the splinter and radical parties.[3] Their participation has been extensive, and their influence in political affairs has been substantial.

Although Indians are statutory citizens, they have had only limited experience in national politics. Their party affiliation is not clear and their political influence is negligible. In recent years the Mexicans have become active in party politics, principally in the Democratic Party. In the Southwest and southern California where they are concentrated, both parties have begun to recognize their potential importance. The Puerto Ricans, Japanese, and Chinese minorities

2. See "Black Candidates Are Winning More Offices Across The South," *The Southern Patriot*, (November, 1972) p. 1.

3. See Nathan Glazer, The Jewish Role in Student Activitism," *Fortune*, 79:122 ff, (January, 1969).

are numerically too small to have exerted any significant influence in the two national parties.

In the major labor unions the minorities have a spotty and undistinguished record. The Indians are largely outside the usual American work force. Jews have been engaged principally in private enterprise and middle-class professional and managerial occupations. A small proportion of Mexicans and blacks are still engaged in unorganized and migratory agricultural jobs. By tradition, many Japanese and Chinese workers are occupied in small business and agricultural enterprises. All these minority workers are included in occupations not covered by major labor unions.

Those blacks who belong to labor unions are concentrated in semi-skilled, low-skilled and service occupations. They dominate a few national unions (e.g., the Brotherhood of Sleeping Car Porters) and they are numerous and influential in other national unions and many union locals. However, in the national labor movement, their numbers, position, and influence remain marginal. The norm of color and the practice of racism have worked to exclude them from the aristocratic craft unions of high skill in construction, production, and service.

The Puerto Ricans, Mexicans, and the Orientals comprise a small and uninfluential sector of the national labor movement. In the main, these workers, when organized, are concentrated in the service unions. Thus, in the aggregate, the place and participation of minorities in organized labor reveals another facet of their inferior and marginal position in the American social structure.

For various reasons, many minority veterans have refused to affiliate with the veterans organizations. This action is an indicator of their sense of alienation from the values and orientations of American society. Most minority persons who have joined veterans organizations find themselves isolated into segregated posts of the inclusive national organizations.

Participation in civic organization is revealed principally at the community level. To a limited extent, civic organizations have state and national dimensions, as in the State Natural Resources Commission or boards of the American Red Cross and United Service Organization. Civic organization refers to the various committees, commissions, and boards that manage the collective life of American communities. Participation is usually by nomination of a community leader or through election by a special constituency.

Two generalizations can be made about this indicator of minorities in American social structure. First, except for the Jews, the minorities are significantly underrepresented and second, where represented, they are concentrated in the lower and less influential ranks.[4]

The situation of Jews in civic organizations is instructive in this connection. John P. Dean found in a study of a middle-size New York community that well-to-do, generous, liberal, and civic-minded Jewish people were very active in community programs.[5] In terms of their numbers they were

4. See William H. Form and Delbert C. Miller, *Industry, Labor and Community* (New York: Harper and Row, 1960), Chapter 7, pp. 248-251.

5. John P. Dean, "Patterns of Socialization and Association Between Jews and Non-Jews," *Jewish Social Studies,* 17:229-51, (July, 1955). Judith Cramer and Semour Levantman, *Children of the Guilded Ghetto* (New Haven: Yale University Press, 1961), pp. 136-37; and Ann C. Balth, ed., *Barriers: Patterns of Discrimination Against Jews,* Anti-Defamation League, 1958, pp. 43-51.

overrepresented on the community's civic bodies. However, Dean also found that Jews were studiously excluded from membership on those committees, commissions, and boards that might require or encourage intimate social associations with top-level dominants of the community. In other words, civic participation functioned to implement the exclusion of Jews from social assimilation, as will be discussed in a later chapter.

Alienation

Ecological and structural separation, and status inferiority support the sense of alienation from American society that is shared by many minority people. This reaction is revealed as a sense of isolation and powerlessness. For example, some studies show that the alleged "voluntary" separation of Jews is in significant measure a reaction against the sense of isolation from dominant society. Thus Albert I. Gordon quotes a middle-class Jewish woman in a metropolitan suburb on the subject as follows:

Jews and Christians do not meet socially, even in suburbia. If we do, you bet that it is to help promote some cause or organization where they think we Jews can be helpful. But after five o'clock there is no social contact, no parties, no visits, no nothing![6]

The sense of isolation is exaggerated and unrelieved among American Indians who have perceived themselves as a group of nations apart from American society. The invasion and ransacking of the Bureau of Indian Affairs in the fall of 1972 and other demonstrations by the American Indian Movement dramatize their feeling of isolation.[7] As they think of themselves and the national society, they can find little ground for consensus and identification.

In the black community the sense of isolation is often identified as polarization. In another place the process of and phenomenon of polarization have been analyzed in the following words:

Ecologically separated, blacks and whites pull away from each other in a gesture that opens the social distance between the two groups and rotates them away from each other. In a decisive turning operation blacks are left facing in toward themselves and away from whites in the general society.[8]

All the minorities experience the sense of powerlessness to varying degrees within the bureaucratic world of the dominant group. The collective perception of powerlessness is accentuated by recent events that have heightened their aspirations and awakened their conviction that change is possible. The political activities of the minorities that are examined in Chapter 5 of this book constitute dramatic evidence of their urgent sense of powerlessness. The idea and slogan of "black power" represents a direct response to the sense of powerlessness among the black masses in metropolitan America.

The cohesive, symbolically sealed-off minority community functions both to sustain the sense of powerlessness and to offer an antidote to this feeling. Chinatown, the barrio, the ghetto, and the black community are defensive mechanisms of people who are sensitive to their vulnerability against

6. Albert I. Gordon, *Jews in Suburbia* (Boston: Beacon, 1959), p. 170, by permission.
7. *New York Times*, November 12, 1972, Section E, p. 5.
8. Joseph S. Himes, *Racial Conflict in American Society* (Columbus: Merrill, 1973), p. 131, by permission.

the dominant white society. At the same time, these minority enclaves are also defensive agents against the established culture of the dominant group.

The location of the minorities within American social structure has at least two significant consequences for social relations with the dominants. Ecological isolation and social subordination of the minorities makes it difficult, if indeed not impossible, for them to maintain democratic relations with the dominants. This is the structural situation for condescension and deference.

Second, geographic isolation and structural inferiority are more likely to foster conflict than cooperation. In later chapters it will be shown that relations between minorities and dominants have always revealed some combination of cooperation and conflict. In recent years the tendency toward conflict has been increased.

SOCIAL ORGANIZATION WITHIN THE MINORITY GROUPS

Social organization can be thought of as that dynamic pattern revealed in the arrangements and relations among the constituents of a social unit. While every social unit has its own internal pattern of organization, at the same time it is a participating constituent in the organization of some larger social unit. Thus, while the dominant group and all the minorities participate in the inclusive organization of American society, each also reveals its own more or less distinctive pattern of organization. In the present discussion, the inclusive organization of American society, as it is qualified by the dominant group, is assumed. This is the social organization discussed in other volumes of this series. At this point, attention is focused on the patterns of organization to be found in the several minority groups.

Several conditions qualify and limit this discussion. First, the minority groups reveal a varied series of distinctive social organizations. Second, all are affected by social conditions among which the following may be the most important:

(1) Unique cultural tradition (e.g., Jewish, southern rural black, or Chinese).
(2) Background experiences within the United States (e.g., slavery, official prejudice and discrimination, gang work).
(3) Present societal situation (e.g., reservation living, regional concentration, restricted acculturation).
(4) Perceived group needs, collective goals, group ideologies and other socio-psychological factors, and
(5) The constant and debilitating influence of the norm of color and culture.

And third, the minority groups reveal systems of organization that differ in their capacities to fulfill perceived group needs and/or to meet all societal expectations. Since it will be impossible to describe all the social organizations of the seven minorities in the available space, we will characterize and compare them by sketches of their religious, community and family patterns.

Religious Organization

Mexicans, Puerto Ricans, Jews, Japanese, and Chinese have inclusive religious organizations. Virtually all Jews belong to the inclusive Hebrew religious organization. Nevertheless, change and specialization tend to limit organizational unity. American Jews are affiliated with three types of synagogues, orthodox, conservative, and reform. While Mexicans and Puerto Ricans are Roman Catholics, they usually belong to distinct nationality parishes. Middle-class Americanized Roman Catholic parishes differ significantly from those composed of recent immigrants from Puerto Rico and Mexico.

With blacks and Indians, religious splintering is basic. Blacks are affiliated with an aggregation of Protestant denominations and sects. A few blacks are Catholic parishioners or members of non-American alien sects. The American Indian tribes reveal a bewildering array of different religious and magical systems. Some Indians have been converted to the various prevailing American religions.

The local religious organization enjoys great importance with poor, ill-adjusted, lower-class members of these minorities. The congregation, parish, synagogue, or temple is a basic unit of primary social organization. The priest, minister, or rabbi is more than a religious leader. Religious belief tends to exert strong, though sometimes unpredictable, influences upon social and personal behavior. The local religious organization is a basic sociability and service agency for its members. One result of this close local cohesion is to make religious organization divisive in the larger group.

In most cases, local religious units are connected with inclusive bureaucratic structures. Jewish synagogues or Roman Catholic parishes are affiliated with inclusive national and international organizations. Most black congregations constitute local units of denominational organizations. Thus, while the local organization may exert a divisive influence, the inclusive structure functions to unify the group. The inclusive religious organizations also execute social control and carry out important collective activities for the minority groups. Religious organization is one apparatus for collective action by the minorities.

Community Organization

With the exception of the Indians, the minority populations are predominantly urban and these urban populations are concentrated in the central cities of metropolitan areas. Being middle-class, most Jews live outside central cities, and most of the Indian population lives on reservations. Typically, then, the "black belts," Chinatowns, *colonias,* and other minority communities are in poor central-city areas. These communities are the locale of the minority subcultures discussed in Chapter 4. The large central-city minority communities are connected to satellite settlements scattered in other sections of the metropolis.

Most of these central-city communities reveal a similar basic ecological pattern. The major axis is a "main street" of business, recreation, and collective action. This arterial street is intersected and paralleled by a network of side streets where the people live crowded together without much respect to social class. The minority community is separated from surrounding areas by a vague and shifting boundary line that marks the locale of culture assimilation, minority expansion, and intergroup conflict.

A classic illustration of organization at this level is the traditional black community. Main street (e.g., "Sweet Auburn" in Atlanta, State Street in Chicago, Beal Street in Memphis or Central Avenue in Los

Angeles) is peppered with grocery and drug stores, beauty and barber shops, cafés and bars, poolrooms and night clubs, pawn shops and second-hand stores, storefront churches and mortuaries, real estate and insurance offices, pressing shops and record bars, and offices of doctors, dentists and lawyers, housed in old buildings. Many of the business and professional men are middle-class, but most of their customers, clients, and patrons are from the lower classes. By day the street and shops are thronged with people transacting the ordinary business of their lives; by night with many of the same people out for fun.

Although middle-class and lower-class black people are scattered higgledy-piggledy in the residential streets, they move in separate, voluntary, and intimate sociability circles.[9] Formal clubs, informal party networks, and civic associations comprise the world of middle-class blacks. Lower-class blacks, after returning to the community from work outside, pass their free time in the local "street society," the friendship-kinship networks, or participation in illicit activities of the rackets.

Formal organization of the black community is intersected by class distinctions and revealed at two levels. Churches, schools, and business establishments provide the institutional framework of ordinary social life. The other sphere of organized activity is contained within such associations and agencies as fraternal bodies, labor unions, veterans associations, professional and trade associations, civic organizations, protest groups, and political party units.

Within the black community there is a thicket of semi-organized clubs and cliques of many kinds.[10] These include loose groupings of friends who fish, bowl, hunt, shoot pool, or play bridge or poker together. There are teams of young people affiliated with the character-building and recreational agencies. This informal network also includes the gangs that form part of "street society" and the pal groups of all ages that spring up where people associate together.

Tuck has characterized the Mexican *colonia* in the following way:

On both sides of Monticello Avenue a small Mexican business district has grown up—cafes, grocery stores, *cantinas*, a barber shop, a bakery, a drug store, and a couple of *tortillerías*. The hiring and provisioning agency for the Sante Fe is also here. Much of the life of the Mexican-American colony centers on this street . . .[11]

Urban renewal and model cities have exerted a disorganizing influence on this traditional pattern of the minority community, especially big-city black communities. In order to demolish "substandard" houses, many people have been forced to move to other sectors of the metropolitan area. Long established social systems and networks have been disrupted; and the familiar ecological pattern has been erased.

Most Jews live in middle-class suburbs. The studies have shown that their organiza-

9. See E. Franklin Frazier, *The Negro in the United States* (New York: Macmillan, 1957), pp. 256-61.

10. Nicholas Babchuck and Ralph V. Thompson, "Voluntary Associations of Negroes," *American Sociological Review*, 27:647-55, (October, 1962); and Anthony M. Orrum, "A Reappraisal of the Social and Political Participation of Negroes," *American Journal of Sociology*, 72:32-46, (July, 1967).

11. Ruth D. Tuck, *Not With the Fist* (New York: Harcourt, Brace, Jovanovich, 1946), p. 5, by permission.

tion, with minor exceptions, is similar to that found in other middle-class suburbs.[12] From the outside the Reform Synagogues seem like other middle-class churches, and the Jewish people are involved in business, the professions, the schools and the various civic and service activities. However, close interpersonal relations of the evenings and weekends take place within all-Jewish circles. In this intimate circle of relatives and friends life is qualified by the Jewish subculture.

Those Indians who left the reservations have not established segregated central-city communities. Their numbers are too small and they are too scattered. Though Indian, they are divided by different tribal cultures and backgrounds. Moreover, the urban Indians have opted for life within culturally American localities whenever that is possible.

On the reservations, community organization is conditioned by the heavy and omnipresent hand of the government. As food-gatherers and hunters, the Indians never took to agriculture. They have consequently remained widely dependent on public assistance. Neither possessing nor needing schools to transmit their tribal cultures, "education" has emerged as an artifical, institutionalized mechanism for "Americanizing" the Indians. One of its main consequences has been cultural and social disorganization. Poor, disorganized, and isolated, the Indians have been vulnerable to many health hazards.[13] The federal Public Health Service has responded to this situation with extensive programs. The result of these conditions is weakening of traditional tribal organization, and failure to establish viable substitute patterns.

Family Organization

Minority families are monogamous (one husband-one wife), headed by the father and initiated in a religious ceremony. However, because of diverse nationality or subcultural backgrounds, they differ, both from one another and from the American norm, in organization and ordinary usage. These minority families are changing by both acculturation and upward mobility in the direction of conformity to the middle-class norms.

Most Jewish people are already middle class. Increasing numbers of Japanese, blacks, Puerto Ricans, Chinese and Mexicans are becoming middle class. The family organization and behavior of these people is rather typically American. Traditional male dominance (sometimes extreme) is giving away to husband-wife sharing of status and authority. The large-family tradition is being moderated by the practice of family planning. The high aspiration-education effort-achievement syndrome, traditional in Jewish and Japanese culture, is becoming a central principle in these families. Family members turn outside the kinship circle for peer relations and self expression.

Although these minority groups differ in many ways, because of similar present or folk backgrounds, the lower-class members share certain traits in common. Some of these shared characteristics influence family organization and behavior and tend to

12. Herbert J. Gans, "The Origin and Growth of a Jewish Community in the Suburbs: A Study of the Jews of Park Forest," in *The Jews: Social Patterns of an American Group,* Marshall Sklare, ed. (New York: Free Press, 1968), pp 205-248.

13. See Alvin M. Josephy, Jr., "Wounded Knee and All That," *New York Times Magazine,* (March 18, 1973) pp. 18 ff.

produce typical patterns. These typical family patterns have been embedded in the various subcultures and reveal significant deviations from the American middle-class norms.

Male dominance is almost universal among the lower-class minority peoples. Evident in all spheres of life, it is institutionalized in marriage. With few exceptions, males, men and boys, control top positions and major authority in family, church, and community. The strength of this pattern varies from group to group and tends to diminish with acculturation and upward mobility.

One aspect of male dominance is the *machismo* complex (glorification of male sexual potency.) This pattern conditions relations between men and women in all spheres of life. A reaction to the *machismo* complex in some subcultures is the institution of chaperonage to protect young and unmarried females from predatory males.

Within the minority lower-class tradition, social maturity and marriage come at an early age. As a consequence, education, when available, is limited and the tradition of education is not strong. Male dominance, a *machismo* complex, and early marriage produce large families. The love of children, opposition to birth control even when it is available, and appreciation of children as old—age insurance support the large family pattern. The population consequence of this pattern is the high proportion of children in the minorities that was reported in Chapter 2.

Being poor, lower-class, and minority, these people live in central cities where housing is poor and families are crowded with access to few "amenities." Two family-linked correlates of this situation are poor physical and mental health, and deviations from the middle-class norms. Under such circumstances families maximize patterns of communal living, sharing, social sensitivity, mutual aid, and acceptance of the lack of privacy.

The strength and importance of kinship networks for such lower-class people has been frequently remarked.[14] These networks that link several large families together perform functions that, in middle-class neighborhoods, are discharged by service agencies. Thus such networks are agents of sociability, mutual aid, social control, protection and the like. They constitute direct links from the individual into the inclusive minority society and ultimately the larger national society.

Summary

In this chapter we have examined the position of the minorities in the inclusive social organization and some patterns of organization within the minority groups. The facts of ecological location, education, economic situation, religious activity, formal participation and alienation indicate that, except for the Jews and some individuals in the other groups, the minorities are concentrated in the working and lower classes. At the same time, while the minorities are conforming to the dominant norms, they still reveal divergent patterns of religious, community and family organization.

For Further Reading

Crossland, Fred E. *Minority Access to College*, New York: Schocken, 1971.

14. Frazier, *The Negro in The United States*, pp. 320-21; and Robert B. Hill, *The Strengths of Black Families* (New York: Emerson Hall, 1972).

Examines barriers to college admission of blacks, Mexicans, Indians, etc.

Dean, John P. "Patterns of Socialization and Association between Jews and Non-Jews," *Jewish Social Studies*, Vol. 17, pp. 247-268, (July, 1955).

A critical examination of the place of Jews in the national social structure.

Franklin, John Hope. *From Slavery to Freedom*, New York: Vintage, 1969.

A distinguished history of blacks in American society.

Jacobson, Julius ed., *The Negro and the American Labor Movement*, Garden City: Doubleday Anchor, 1968.

An anthology that examines the roles of blacks in American labor unions.

Kozol, Jonathan. *Death at an Early Age*, Boston: Houghton Mifflin, 1967.

Describes the destruction of the hearts and minds of Negro children in Boston public schools.

Levine, Stuart and Lurie, Nancy O. eds., *The American Indian Today*, Baltimore: Penguin Books, 1968.

The articles probe the present conditions of American Indians.

Moquin, Wayne with Van Doren, Charles. *A Documentary History of the Mexican Americans*, New York: Bantam Books, 1972.

A comprehensive picture of the "forgotten Americans," from 1936 to 1970.

4 | The Minority Subcultures

THE preceding chapters have shown that minority groups are characterized by racial and cultural traits that distinguish them from the dominant group and that are held in low esteem by members of that group. These deviant cultural traits vary among the different minorities and derive from several sources. They tend to be adjusted to selected features of the dominant American culture in adaptive systems that are called subcultures.

In terms of the source of the deviant elements, we can distinguish two types of minority subcultures. One type, like that of the American blacks, consists of a mixture of indigenous improvisations and dominant cultural patterns. Although largely American in origin, it is nonetheless different from the culture of the dominant white group. The other type is a mixture of alien traits imported by immigrants and elements of the dominant pattern. These are the subcultures of the nationality minorities, for example, Mexican or Chinese.

These subcultures are parts of the inclusive American cultural heritage. They are sufficiently similar to the dominant pattern to be recognized as American. At the same time, they are different enough to be per-

ceived as minority patterns and sources of minority visibility.

Within the American social system, these subcultures perform several social functions. First, they support minority classification and treatment of certain peoples by the dominant group. Second, the subcultures facilitate cohesion within the various minorities. Mutual recognition, the sense of "we" and the capacity to act collectively are supported by the group's subculture. Third, the various subcultures constitute a source of conflict between minorities and the dominant group. This topic is examined in Chapter 5. And fourth, the concept and fact of subcultures establishes a basis for minority-group ideologies and for one theory of societal integration.

THE SUBCULTURES

What a Subculture Is

For our purpose, a subculture can be thought of as a variant of an inclusive national culture which identifies the group or category that practices it as a member of the inclusive national society, while differentiating it from the dominant group. All of the racial and ethnic minorities possess subcultures. In every case these subcultures also reveal a mixture of dominant American elements and deviant traits. The proportions of dominant and deviant constituents and the nature of the deviant elements vary among the minority groups. American blacks reveal the largest proportion of dominant traits while reservation Indians retain the highest proportion of deviant elements.

Three principle types of traits make up the core of the dominant culture found in every subculture. First, the subcultures are grounded in the American core values.[1] These include such items as individual freedom, equality of opportunity, social justice, the free personality, and the central importance of the individual. In accepting and promoting these values the minority groups are American. In this way also they participate in the consensus of the society.

Instrumental bureaucratic patterns comprise the second set of dominant traits in the minority subcultures. These are the norms and values of the job ,education, government, commercial activity, legal behavior and the like. The minorities must learn and practice these patterns in order to survive within the formal American system. They are the skills that are first acquired in the course of learning American culture.

The third dominant component of the minority subcultures, called "mass culture," is the cluster of popular patterns that "mask" or "film" over social differences. These patterns include, among others, vernacular language, commercial art, the world of advertising, realms of personnal conduct, the spheres of style, and so on. In the world of mass culture, dominants and minorities are all one size and kind of Americans.

Three major categories of traits compose the deviant sector of the minority subcultures. Perhaps the most obvious is language. One striking dimension of acculturation is the acquisition, as second language, by immigrants and as native language by their children, of the American version of the English language. Although English is the native language for American blacks, for many it tends to deviate from dominant patterns in both vocabulary and pronunciation.

Second, religion is another sphere of cultural deviation from dominant whites. The Roman Catholicism of the Mexicans and Puerto Ricans is deviant insofar as it has not yet become "Americanized" as Will Herberg has said.[2] Religious practices of the Orientals and American Indians differ radically from those of the dominant American faiths. In the case of all these groups, religion is a source of minority visibility.

American blacks are typically Protestant. However, segregation has produced black religious institutions and patterns that deviate from the Protestant norm. The "black church" supports minority visibility of the group.

Family and community are the locale of the third type of deviant traits in the minority subcultures. In the case of the immigrant groups—Jews, Mexicans, Puerto Ricans, Chinese and Japanese—patterns of kinship and primary relations were brought from alien homelands. Family and community norms of the Indians are elements of tribal cultures surviving under the conditions of reservation living. After generations of living under conditions of segregation

1. Joseph S. Himes, *The Study of Sociology* (Glenview, Ill.: Scott, Foresman, 1968), p. 90.
2. Will Herberg, *Protestant-Catholic-Jew* (Garden City: Doubleday, 1955).

and rejection, blacks have developed networks of primary relationship patterns that differentiate them from the dominant whites.

SUBCULTURES ILLUSTRATED

The racial and ethnic subcultures reflect great variety. For example, the American Indians encompass a great mixture of quasi-independent culture systems. On the other hand, since blacks are indigenous Americans and since in recent generations they have known no other culture, it is difficult to discover the traits that are not American. It may prove useful to examine briefly some of these subcultures in detail.

Jewish Subculture

Whatever distinguishes the Jewish minority is a result of culture, not of biology. The range of variations within Jewish subculture is rather extreme, certainly in respect to some traits and areas. Therefore the picture presented here is "typical," a kind of average.[3]

Perhaps the dominating feature of Jewish subculture is the Hebrew religion. In Jewish life, religion embraces the inclusive organization and the local synagogue, the centrality of the Old Testament and Talmud, the unique status of the rabbi, and the influence of religion on intellectualism, personal conduct, and family-community life. The religious dimension of the subculture varies from the strict orthodoxy of the Hasidic sects to the Americanized patterns of reform synagogues.

The Jewish subculture is characterized by an appreciation of intellectualism. In business this orientation is revealed as shrewdness, or the rational calculation of risks and opportunities in relation to the possible outcomes of action. This orientation turns young Jews toward the professions, humanities, social studies, and the arts. It gives direction to endeavor and achievement in Jewish life.

For millennia the Jews have been a migratory people. One consequence is inclination toward Zionism. While every Jew is established within the society, he is also ambivalent with respect to the issue of "home;" he is a Zionist.

Perhaps the most pervasive aspect of Jewish subculture is the fabric and texture of family and neighborhood life. At this level, Jewish life is characterized by warm intimacy, mutual support, respect for elders, and strong cohesion. The Yiddish language, kosher foods, and the other unique traits of Jewish life are part of the family-neighborhood pattern. At this level the subculture includes the round of ceremonies that involve the individual (child and adult), the progression through stages of society, the strong sense of accountability and wider civic responsibility. Values and norms of this kind contribute to low delinquency rates, strong family and community organization, outstanding academic performance, vigorous civic activity, and solid achievement in most spheres of endeavor.

Mexican Subculture

The subculture of the Mexican-Americans is qualified by the Spanish language,

3. George E. Simpson and J. Milton Yinger, *Racial and Cultural Minorities* (New York: Harper and Row, 1972), pp. 300-02, 480-83, 541-45. And Charles F. Marden and Gladys Meyer, *Minorities in American Society*, (New York: American Book Company, 1968), pp. 410-11, 414-17.

Roman Catholicism, and a sense of "peoplehood," as Milton M. Gordon puts it.[4] This pattern is one manifestation of that inclusive syndrome that is said to characterize "la raza" (the Latin-American racial people).[5] The immigrant Mexicans are Spanish speaking, although their children often become bilingual. Life in family and *barrio* (neighborhood) is lived in Spanish. It cannot be translated easily—for it encompasses networks and levels of interpersonal relations that can be expressed only in the Spanish language.

In the Southwest and Southern California the subculture is interwoven with the structures, authority, and rituals of the Mexican Catholic church. Among first and second generations, Catholicism is a salient element of daily life. The power of religion and the *padre* control most aspects of life; and the thread of religious belief runs through the collective sense of destiny, acceptance of things as they are.

The subculture is strongly qualified by the folk texture of intimate life in family and *barrio*. Male dominance and the value of manliness are expressed in male leadership, the honor of men, sense of responsibility, and male sexual virility or *machismo*. Family and *barrio* are the locale of an inclusive war—network of intimate communications and relations that support and protect all members of the community. This network embraces all members in the warm, sensuous experience of peoplehood and so differentiates them from their anglo neighbors.

The Black Subculture

The subculture of American blacks has come to be known as "*soul*."[6] This term refers to the value themes and norms that qualify the religious, family, and community life of blacks, that distinguish them culturally from the white dominants. *Soul* can be analyzed in terms of three elemental components: spirituality, feeling, and spontaneity.[7]

Perhaps the most authentic expression of *soul* is religion. The forms and patterns of worship provide channels for the expression of spirituality, feeling, and spontaneity. The cadences, imagery, and intonations of preaching, the spontaneity of feeling in shouted response, and the rhythms and harmonies of song, are expressions of *soul*.

Play among blacks is another manifestation of *soul*. Here spontaneity and feeling are clearly expressed. The play life of blacks, though it may take place within the confines of traditional and organized games and sports, is nevertheless a marvel of the interplay of feelings and the freshness of improvisations. Often, the uninitiated can hardly differentiate religious expression from play activity. Both function to communicate *soul*, and the modes of expression reveal many similarities.

The music of blacks is an authentic facet for the expression of *soul*. Several unique folk forms have arisen within the black tradition. The better known are spirituals, blues, jazz, and gospel. Songs in these

4. Milton M. Gordon, *Assimilation in American Life* (New York: Oxford, 1964), pp. 23-24.

5. William Madsen, *The Mexican Americans of South Texas* (New York: Holt, Rinehart and Winston, 1964), p. 18.

Marden and Meyer, *Minorities in American Society* p. 134.

6. Joseph S. Himes, *Racial Conflict in American Society* (Columbus: Merrill, 1973), Chapter 4; and Joseph S. Himes, "Negro Teen Age Culture," *The Annals* 338:91-101 (November 1961).

7. Himes, *Racial Conflict*, pp. 88-91.

modes may be traditional, or composed for the commercial market. They are sacred and secular, but the distinctions sometimes can be recognized only by means of the words. That is, a soulful lament may sob about unrequited love or about the suffering of Jesus.

One can also wear *soul*. Forms of dress and personal adornment constitute still other expressions of *soul*. The hair styles for men and women called "Afro" and "natural" are cases in point. Styles of shirts, pants, and jackets (fatigues "dashikis," "Nehru" and black leather jackets), have been borrowed and adapted. Beads, chains, ribbons, shoes, and the rest have also been installed in the corpus of adornment usage that constitutes *soul*. A further aspect of this expression is the penchant of some black people for bright, sometimes incongruous colors. Such colors respond to and facilitate the expression of feelings and moods.

The *soul* look is all those things and practices that serve to accentuate or highlight distinctive Negroid racial traits. It draws attention to the black skin, the kinky or frizzy hair, the broad flat nose, and the thick lips. It also dramatizes distinctive postures, gaits and motor action patterns of black people. The soul look is the black look. It says, "Yes, see, I'm black. Black is good. Black is beautiful."

"Soul food" is the culinary expression of spirit and improvisation in the life of blacks. It includes that collection of recipes and dishes that became established in the black tradition during the lean days of the Civil War and Reconstruction. They feature parts left over from the butchering of swine, namely feet, hamhocks, tails, ears, intestines (chitterlings); greens, both cultivated and wild; corn products; peas; beans; and the like. These simple items became "soul food" through the magic of methods of preparation, seasoning, and cooking that distill from them subtle and tantalizing aromas and flavors.

Soul talk is a world of argot and modes of expression that lock blacks into the black community and function to exclude whites. It includes a unique set of patterns of phrasing, cadence, enunciation, and intonation. Within this inclusive communication system one recognizes subpatterns of expression, "jive," or modes of kidding and flattery, talking "trash," or "junk"; "cursing," and "playing the dozens", or the art of aggression through disparaging remarks and intimations about one's close relatives. There is a style of soul talk for most situations, e.g., for church, for the men's informal gathering in the barbershop, for the protest meeting.

In the racially hostile society, community and family have been havens for protection, support and warmth for blacks. Intimate norms facilitate the expression of soul in kinship, religious, and neighborhood settings. The constraints of segregation, discrimination, and impotence support deviant modes of community and family organization and collective action for values that have special meaning in the black world. These values are often personified in the heroes and villains that comprise an important part of black history and folklore.

ASSIMILATING THE SUBCULTURES

During the colonial and early national periods, the white Anglo-Saxon Protestants controlled the society and set the cultural norm. The resident "outsiders" and later immigrants (e.g., the Dutch, Germans, Swedes, Indians and blacks), were expected to conform to this cultural norm. The white outsiders could aspire to join the dominant Anglo-American group; but the Indians and blacks were excluded from group membership by the norms of color and culture. In this drama of conforming and joining, the white outsiders were expected to learn how to be Americans to qualify for acceptance into the dominant group. Such a conception of the assimilation process defined relations between minorities and dominants in terms of cooperation and integration.

Conformity

From the outset people tended to see the process of assimilation in two somewhat different ways; as conformity to the Anglo-American cultural norm, or as reciprocal bio-cultural fusion in a societal melting pot.[8] The route of conformity required outsiders to give up their native cultures and to accept the Anglo-American complex. As a consequence, the dominants suspected and discouraged the development of rural and urban nationality communities, and strove to prevent the formation and stabilization of ethnic subcultures. Assimilation by conformity held out the implied hope that those whites who successfully mastered the Anglo-American culture might also be accepted into the dominant group.

When most immigrants were coming from Northwestern Europe and belonged to cultures that were basically similar to the Anglo-American pattern, assimilation by conformity worked with some success. Later, however, during the last half of the nineteenth and first quarter of the twentieth centuries, when most immigrants were coming from Southeastern Europe and Asia, the assimilation process failed to fuse them into the society. In this situation, to facilitate the process, "Americanization" programs (i.e, consciously organized assimilation activities) were established by some industries, patriotic organizations, settlement houses, and the like. Yet, even with these efforts it proved impossible to assimilate the great horde of people with alien ways that kept coming. Discouraged and alarmed, some people saw the "new" immigrants as unassimilable and called for restriction of immigration. In the 1920s the United States officially acknowledged the failure of assimilation by conformity through passage of restrictive immigration legislation.

In spite of this gesture of frustration and defeat, we might ask: How far did the policy and ideology of assimilation by conformity to the Anglo-American cultural norm succeed? We can formulate the answer to this question by examining three levels of assimilation. At the first level, called "survival assimilation," outsiders acquire the norms and values required for existing within the society. These include, among others, language, morals, money skills, travel practices, job ways, shopping knowledge, and the minimal social techniques required for ordinary social intercourse. The number and variety of such cultural ways will differ with the individual's situation. For example, a man who resides within a nationality ghetto, barrio, or other community and goes out each day to work will need and learn more ways of his new society than his wife who passes most of her time within the confines of the ethnic locality.

8. Cordon, *Assimilation,* 84-131.

At the survival level, it can be said that assimilation by conformity succeeded. The Anglo-American pattern is virtually unchallenged as the cultural norm save in a few isolated enclaves.

At the second level of assimilation by conformity, here called "bureaucratic integration," people gain entrance into the roles and statuses of the major bureaucratic institutions and learn the cultural lore that attaches to these roles. In the economy, this means the ranks of activity and authority beyond unskilled labor; in government, performance of roles of all kinds beyond that of machine-controlled bloc voter. These assimilating people participate in education, welfare, religion, the military, recreation, etc., as consumer-clients, workers and administrators of all types. Integration into the bureaucracies reflects the process of upward mobility that occurs simultaneously with cultural assimilation. Through such structural movement people are assimilated to most aspects of the Anglo-American complex. The significant exceptions are those roles and statuses that carry with them intimate association with the elites of the dominant group and access to the cultural lore of these elites.

At the bureaucratic integration level, assimilation has been selectively successful. The children of white European immigrants have succeeded at bureaucratic integration. Some white immigrants are held back by their ethnic culture; non-whites by both their culture and their color. The bureaucratic restrictions rest lightest upon mainland-born white and mulatto Puerto Ricans, the American-born and educated Japanese and Chinese. The burdens of discrimination are heaviest upon immigrant Mexicans,

Puerto Ricans, Chinese, and Japanese, and upon blacks and Indians of all stations.

The third level of assimilation by conformity, called "social assimilation" refers to full acceptance of the children of the newcomers into the elite ranks of the dominant group. Acceptance is indicated by membership and participation in clubs and cliques, by residence in elite neighborhoods, by the exchange of dinner and party invitations, and by intermarriage. Social assimilation also means internalization of the values and norms that are unique to the dominant group.

Assimilation is most restricted at this level. With the passage of the generations, many members of non-English white European groups have been absorbed into the dominant group at the bureaucratic integration level. However, most immigrant whites (whether from Northern or Southern Europe), Jews and many Roman Catholics and their children have been excluded from social assimilation.[9] Very few members of the non-white minorities have been socially assimilated in this way.

The Melting Pot

The other route of assimilation that appeared early in our national history is the "melting pot" process.[10] Its most recent statement was in Oscar Handlin's *The Newcomers*.[11] *The melting pot* is an extreme formulation of the idea of taking newcomers into the society by assimilating them.

9. John P. Dean, "Patterns of Socialization and Association Between Jews and Non-Jews," *Jewish Social Studies*, 17:247-68, (July, 1955).

10. Gordon, *Assimilation*, pp. 115-131.

11. Oscar Handlin, *The Newcomers* (Cambridge: Harvard University Press, 1959).

The process envisages the young and growing nation as a huge bio-social caldron wherein a great variety of divergent biological stocks and cultural heritages are melted down and blended together in a new societal mix. Unlike assimilation by conformity, the melting-pot formula sees assimilation by reciprocity. Both the Anglo-American cultural complex and all other heritages are melted down, reformed, modified, and blended together. What comes out of the melting pot is a new American culture, composed of a blend of all the materials that went into it.

At the same time, the melting-pot process envisages biological amalgamation. The biological stocks will blend and be fused by intermarriage. A new American "race" will emerge.

As Milton Gordon points out, this idea was advanced with feeling and eloquence. However, it never had much impact on the process of American life because its tenets violate the norm of culture and color. For cultures to be fused and blended, the Anglo-American complex must give way in part to heritages from other lands. This expectation contradicts the ethnocentric requirement of Anglo conformity.[12] At the same time, the demands of the melting pot violate the norm of color. It would open the gates to amalgamation with non-white stocks such as blacks, Indians and the Orientals.

The melting pot idea has undergone several refinements during the last half century. Frederick Jackson Turner employed the concept as a major device for explaining the role of the frontier in American history.[13] In Turner's opinion the melting pot is a process of frontier and rural life. Later, August Hollingshead, from a study of intermarriage in New Haven, demonstrated that

the melting pot has been an essential process of urban life.[14] Later Ruby Joe Reeves Kennedy identified a "triple" melting pot in New Haven.[15] She found evidence of nationality intermarriage within the three religions, i.e., Protestant, Catholic, and Jewish. Thus Irish and Italians or Germans and Scandinavians might intermarry. In this way these nationality groups are blended in the bio-cultural melting pot. However, she found that there was little intermarriage among the three religious groups. The three melting pots were thus intra-religious but cross-national.

This research suggests that the melting-pot mechanism seems to make limited contribution to the assimilation of alien peoples to the Anglo-American bio-cultural base. Whatever cultural assimilation takes place in the melting pot is explained mainly as conformity to the Anglo-American norm. The biological fusion that takes place is restricted and determined by the important boundaries of group life within the American social structure. In the end though, the deviant racial and cultural minorities remain largely unassimilated.

Conclusion

The study of assimilation in American life leads us to three conclusions. First, after

12. Stewart G. and Mildred W. Cole, *Minorities and the American Promise* (New York: Harper and Row, 1954), Chapter 6.

13. Frederick Jackson Turner, *The Frontier in American History* (New York: Holt, Rinehart and Winston, 1920).

14. August B. Hollingshead, "Cultural Factors in the Selection of Marriage Mates," *American Sociological Review,* 15:619-27, (October 1950).

15. Ruby Joe Reeves Kennedy, "Single or Triple Melting Pot? Intermarriage in New Haven, 1870-1950, *American Journal of Sociology,* 58:56-59, (July, 1952).

three centuries the diverse American minorities remain largely unassimilated. At the level of survival, assimilation is almost universal. At the level of bureaucratic integration, assimilation is relatively advanced but selective. But at the level of social assimilation the minorities remain largley excluded from American life.

Second, the more the minority members resemble the Anglo-American model, the more readily they are assimilated. And by the same token, the more they deviate, the greater the resistance to their assimilation.

And third, despite a long-standing national commitment to cultural assimilation, subcultures still characterize the situation of the racial and ethnic minorities. A policy for the future must be sought with the fact of minority subcultures as one salient ingredient.

With these conclusions before us, it will be instructive to examine the idea of cultural pluralism. Many individuals and groups of outsiders and newcomers actively sought assimilation into the Anglo-American dominant sector. Others rejected this course of action and preferred retention of their native cultures and ways of life. From the outset, the non-white people recognized that assimilation was inaccessible to them. In time the reactions against assimilation were formalized into the concept of "pluralism."[16] This approach to the issue of the divergent peoples took two somewhat different forms which are here called "societal pluralism" and cultural pluralism."

Societal Pluralism

Even before the Revolutionary War, rural enclaves of nationality and religious immigrants began to appear. Later there were settlements of Germans in Ohio, and Swedes and Norwegians in Minnesota and the Dakotas, religious groups like the Amish in Pennsylvania, the Amana in Iowa, and Menonites in several states; and utopian settlements of various kinds. These separatist groups found living room and social tolerance in the uncrowded woods and prairie lands of the western states and territories.

They wanted to avoid absorption into the Anglo-American body and to maintain their cultural identities. This meant maintaining the integrity of their culture and preventing its contamination. They undertook to defend the close-knit cohesion of their group by preventing both in-migration of strangers and out-migration of members. They controlled marriage, thus preventing group mixing. And finally, they sought in various ways to establish and maintain a substantial degree of political and quasi-political autonomy. For example, they defended their right to control the settlement of small disputes and to regard their local norms as having the validity of common law. They envisaged the American society as an inclusive interdependent series of large and small societal enclaves, ordered and directed by the national government.

Toward the end of the nineteenth century societal pluralism began to decline. The growth of large industrial cities tended to lure young members away from the confines of the ancestral sub-societies. The improvement of transportation, the growth of trade, the development of public education, the spread of "popular democracy," as well as other developments, forced cultural in-

16. See William M. Newman, *American Pluralism* (New York: Harper and Row, 1973), Chapter 3.

cursions from the outside into these hitherto relatively impervious enclaves. The opportunity for assimilation into the dominant group proved irresistible to some young ambitious members. From the outset, the federal government opposed the possibility of weakening the national solidarity by this trend toward societal fragmentation.

Cultural Pluralism

In the latter years of the nineteenth and early decades of the twentieth centuries, pluralism began to reveal another form. It appeared as an urban phenomenon characteristic of the aggregations of immigrants from Southern and Eastern Europe. Its appearance paralleled the stabilization of the minority subcultures and the desperate struggles of these minorities for social survival against the attacks of the "Americanization" programs.

In the earlier section of this chapter, we suggested the nature of the cultural pluralism model. It envisages an inclusive American culture dominated by the Anglo-American pattern, and characterized by a series of deviations around this mode. One set of deviations is comprised of the various minority subcultures (e.g., Jewish, black, Oriental, Spanish language, and American Indian). Another type of variants around the Anglo-American mode includes the specialized subcultures (e.g., class, regional, occupational, religious, and so on). This is the societal model for which the slogan "diversity within unity" is appropriate.

Recent development in relations with the American Indians have revived serious consideration of societal pluralism.[17] For some time Indian leaders and organizations had been demanding "self-determination" for the reservations. In 1970 President Nixon embraced self-determination as the keystone of his policy recommendations for revamping the complex government relations with the Indians. However, following a burst of enthusiastic effort, progress toward this end was slowed by failure of the Congress to pass the necessary legislation, and by obstructions of key governmental officials. This made the Indians restive; in the early 1970s young Indians, mainly from the cities and under the auspicies of the militant American Indian Movement, began a series of extremist and violent incidents that climaxed at Wounded Knee, South Dakota in March, 1973. Their demands for change were couched in a list of twenty points in which self-determination was the key item. In the negotiations with the government that accompanied and followed these events, societal pluralism in the guise of local self-determination was revived as a viable arrangement for patterning relations with the Indians.

Summary

From the outset the Anglo-American dominants assumed that newcomers would learn their culture. This assimilation took two forms called Anglo-American conformity and the melting pot. However, neither process succeeded very well. Meanwhile, in spite of considerable pressure, the minorities clung to their old ways and developed a series of racial and ethnic subcultures. In the end, foreign immigration was virtually terminated; society permitted the minorities to retain their subcultures under an ar-

17. See Alvin M. Josephy, "Wounded Knee and All That," *New York Times Magazine* (March 18, 1973) pp, 18 ff.

rangement called cultural or societal pluralism.

For Further Reading

Carmichael, Stokeley and Hamilton, Charles V. *Black Power*, New York: Vintage, 1967.

One statement of the pluralism point of view.

Gordon, Milton M. *Assimilation in American Life*, New York: Oxford, 1964.

The definitive study of the nature and role of assimilation.

Handlin, Oscar. *Race and Nationality in American Life*, Garden City: Doubleday Anchor, 1957.

A history of the emerging consciousness of race in American life.

Kitano, Harry H. L. *Japanese Americans*, Englewood Cliffs: Prentice-Hall, 1969.

A competent study of the Japanese subculture by a Japanese scholar.

Ludwig, Edward W. and Santibanez, James eds., *The Chicanos*, Baltimore: Penguin Books, 1971.

An anthology by Mexicans about Mexican culture and life.

Newman, William M. *American Pluralism*, New York: Harper and Row, 1973.

An examination of the nature and role of pluralism in American life.

Sklare, Marshall. *Conservative Judaism*, New York: Schocken Books, 1972.

An excellent study of Jewish religion by a competent scholar.

Yinger, J. Milton. *A Minority Group in American Society*, New York: McGraw-Hill, 1965.

A short paperback examination of the culture and social organization of blacks in the United States.

5 | The Politics of Minority Status

MOST discussions of racial and ethnic relations have tended to stress assimilation and cooperation and to minimize antagonism and conflict. Yet antagonism and conflict are as characteristic of these relations as assimilation and cooperation. Conflict in minority-dominant relations arises from the intersecting of the basic values of equality and democracy by the structural conditions of inferiority and exclusion. The strong motivation to struggle by the minorities is restrained within "tolerated" limits by the authority of the dominants.

However, since the mid-50's the level and direction of conflict in these group relations have altered dramatically. All the minority groups, and especially the blacks, have taken the initiative and transformed racial and ethnic relations into one of the most critical problems of the national society. It can be said that racial and ethnic relations are conflict relations.

The task of this chapter is to examine the heightened levels and altered direction of this social conflict. The perspective of our approach is expressed in the phrase "the politics of minority status," for we wish to focus on the aggressive struggles of minority people to modify their inferior status within the society. In the first part of the chapter we will sketch the organized struggles of the minority peoples since the mid-50s. These struggles are seen as the collective response to the traditional segregation, discrimination, and aggression on the part of the dominants. In the second main section of the chapter we will try to identify and describe the conflict styles espoused by the minority groups. In the final section an attempt will be made to explain this conflict and to assess the course of its development in the foreseeable future.

The Black Revolt

In the latter part of the nineteenth century, southern whites struggled by every means at their disposal to eliminate the changes produced by the Civil War. By early in the twentieth century they had returned rural blacks to virtual slave status. However, in the two decades between 1905 and 1925, four national organizations, (the National Association for The Advancement of Colored People, the National Urban League, the Commission on Interracial Cooperation and the Universal Negro Improvement Association) and three dominating leaders (W.E.B. DuBois, Booker T. Washington, and Marcus Garvey) rose to challenge the direction of conflict and to intensify the struggle among blacks.[1] For the next thirty years the conflict was a stand-off, punctuated periodically by violent aggressive white riots and steady but gradual gains by blacks.

Suddenly, between 1954 and 1960, the tide of aggression swung from the whites to the blacks. This reversal of directions and accentuation of intensity was signaled by three dramatic events—the Supreme Court decision of May 17, 1954, banning segregation in public schools; the Montgomery (Alabama) bus boycott of 1955-56; and the black college students sit-ins of 1960.

In terms of the strategy and tactics of struggle, the ensuing conflict evolved in three stages. The first stage can be thought of as lasting roughly from 1955 to 1964. This was the era of non-violent, mass-participating, direct action that was led by Martin Luther King.[2] It was focused in the South and mounted a frontal attack on institutionalized segregation and discrimination. Collective conflict was acted out in boycotts, sit-ins, silent marches, demonstrations, freedom rides, bloc voting, and the like. This era can be thought of as ending with the March on Washington in 1963, and passage of the Civil Rights Act of 1964.

The second period, lasting from 1964 to 1969, was the time of violence. It was ushered in by crystallization of the "black power" theme, the murder of three civil rights workers in Mississippi, and beginning of the aggressive black riots in the summer of 1964. New black leaders (Stokely Carmichael, H. "Rap" Brown, Floyd McKissick) arose to challenge King and engineer the swing from nonviolent to extremist and violent tactics. These were the years of the riots, student take-over of university buildings, threatening confrontations, and inflammatory rhetoric. In half a decade, the fires of violent fury seemed to burn themselves out, and the face of conflict turned toward other approaches within the boundaries of traditional collective action.

Beginning in the late 1960s blacks began to put more stress on their struggle through party politics. Several developments, not connected with racial conflict as such, seem to have facilitated this change. Astute black politicians began to notice that the central cities of the nation's major metropolitan areas were becoming all-black islands. This condition resulted from suburban flight of the whites and steady growth of the black population.[3] These leaders began to organize and manipulate this concentrated black political power, getting themselves elected to city halls, county courthouses, state legislatures, and the Congress. Also it became evident that this concentrated black political power might constitute a major tool in the continuing struggle.

Mexicans, Indians, and Puerto Ricans

In the 1960s and 1970s Mexicans, Indians, and Puerto Ricans joined in the new politics of protest. Struggle did not emerge in the same way and at the same pace in each of these groups, yet in every case it followed prior frustrating experiences with the tactics of moderation and conformity. The protest activity of these minorities is evidence

1. Joseph S. Himes, *Racial Conflict in American Society* (Columbus: Merrill, 1973), Chapter 2.
2. *Ibid.*, Chapter 3.
3. See Joseph S. Himes, "Some Characteristics of the Migration of Blacks in the United States," *Social Biology*, 18:359-366, (December, 1971).

of the bitter conflict associated with racial and ethnic relations.

The Mexicans have been organizing and acting collectively for self-help and protection for a long time.[4] The *Alianza Hispano-Americano* was established in 1840. During the next 50 years, scores of other regional, state and local organizations sprang up throughout the Southwest and West where the Mexicans were concentrated. These early organizations tended to be conservative in approach. They sponsored self-help projects for both barrios and individuals, programs to reduce intergroup tension and discrimination, and activities to facilitate acculturation of the Mexican newcomers.

Following the Second World War, in the middle and late 1940s young Mexicans, especially veterans, began to establish and lead more politically oriented and militant organizations. The G. I. Forum made a special appeal to Mexican veterans. *PASSO* (Political Association of Spanish Speaking Americans) in Texas and *MAPA* (Mexican American Political Association) in California picked up the political militancy torch. In the 1950s, Mexican youth began to stir and to organize for action. Their main agencies were *La Raza Unida* and the Mexican American Youth Organization. Perhaps the best known Mexican action group is Cesar Chavez's National Farm Workers Association. Late in the 1960s, hundreds of regional, state, and local organizations of all ages and ideologies were coordinated by the Congress of Mexican American Unity.

Although these organizations revealed a wide range of ideologies, strategies, and tactics, they tended to show the Mexicans as typically moderate in their protest style. The use of the hyphenation, "Mexican-American," suggests an orientation toward

pluralistic integration. It was often claimed that both by temperament and by tradition Mexican people are non-violent and neighborly. The main thrust of their protest effort is fair treatment, social justice, and equal opportunity in the complex economic and political systems of American national society.

The Indians found it difficult to organize for struggle in the modern political manner. Isolated and scattered on scores of reservations, they were separated from one another by differences of language, customs, and the sense of independent nationhood.[5] Having first been defeated and subjugated by the whites, they were brought under firm control by the national government. By destroying their ancestral hunting and gathering economies, the government transformed the Indians into dependents. One initial reaction to these collective traumas was the series of revivalistic and millenary movements that swept through the Indian reservations during the end of the last and the beginning of the present centuries.

The first Indian organizations for protection and self-help tended to be conservative in outlook.[6] One of the early organizations was the National Congress of American Indians, which worked for reduction of dis-

4. Charles F. Marden and Gladys Meyer, *Minorities in American Society* (New York: American Book Company, 1968), pp. 145-146; and George E. Simpson and J. Milton Yinger, *Racial and Cultural Minorities: An Analysis of Prejudice and Discrimination* (New York: Harper and Row 1972), pp. 712-713.

5. See Alvin M. Josephy, "Wounded Knee and All That: What the Indians Want," *New York Times Magazine*, (March 18, 1973) pp. 18 ff.

6. Simpson and Yinger, *Racial and Cultural Minorities*, pp. 215-16, 413, and 713-15.

New York Times, Section E-5, (November 12, 1972) p. 18.

crimination, self improvement, facilitation of acculturation, and improvement of relations between Indians and whites. Taking both encouragement and example from the black revolt, some young militant Indians established the National Indian Youth Council. The modern era of Indian protest can be said to have begun with the American Indian Chicago Conference of 1961. At this meeting, all the ideological themes of Indian life, from assimilation to political independence surfaced, but the dominant tone was militant action.

Since 1969, the militant young Indians have engaged in a series of tactical activities which belong to what may be called the "politics of visibility." In that year they invaded the Alcatraz Island prison facility and occupied it for several weeks. Later, another band squatted atop the Teddy Roosevelt sculpture in Mt. Rushmore National Park, South Dakota. On November 2, 1972, members of the American Indian Movement invaded the Washington headquarters of the Bureau of Indian Affairs and stayed until promised some high-level attention to their problems. During March and April, 1973, members of the American Indian Movement invaded and occupied Wounded Knee, South Dakota, in a dramatic action for change.[7]

Tactics like those described above had the following primary aims for the Indians:

1. To gain high-level and national attention for their causes and claims.
2. To publicize the abuses and discriminations they felt they had endured and to mobilize supporting public opinion.
3. To initiate remedial action, preferably at the highest level of government, to improve their situation.

The Puerto Ricans are concentrated in northern metropolitan areas, especially in the Northeast. Almost half the million and a half now in the continental United States live in New York City. For some years following the large in-migration of the 1940s there had been organized programs among the Puerto Ricans aimed at facilitating their adjustment to big-city life as well as the acculturation of newcomers, and reducing discrimination by mainland whites.[8] A leading organization was the Citizens Committee for Unity, which had programs to improve neighborhood conditions, aid needy individuals, and provide better relations with the other people in the large eastern cities, especially New York.

After 1968, collective activity in Puerto Rican neighborhoods took a turn toward militancy. In New York, this new approach was spearheaded by the City-wide Action Movement and by the Young Lords. This latter group tried to fashion its tactics after their conception of the Black Panther Party. In Boston, action for social change was led by the Emergency Tenants Council, and in Chicago the leading organization in the Puerto Rican community was *Comunidad Latin*. In all these places and organizations, the thrust of protest was for structural change and altered power relations.

Jews, Japanese, and Chinese

If one is tempted to conclude this narrative of minority protest by asserting that the Jews, Japanese, and Chinese have not, at

7. Alvin M. Josephy, Jr., "Wounded Knee and All That," pp. 18 ff.

8. Simpson and Yinger, *Racial and Cultural Minorities*, p. 413.

least not yet, joined the new politics of militant overt action, such a statement is not altogether accurate, since some members of each of these minority groups are engaged in the new forms of collective struggle. It can be said that typically these minorities have continued to approach their problems in traditionally moderate and conservative ways. Whatever the nature of their approach, however, there can be no doubt that as minority groups Jews, Japanese, and Chinese oppose the derogations and discriminations of their situation in American society.[9]

The Jews have been organized for more than half a century for self-help and protection. Throughout the nineteenth century they encountered waves of anti-Semitism that never permitted them to relax completely. The Anti-Defamation League of B'nai B'rith may be the best known of these organizations. Other well-staffed and active organizations include the American Jewish Congress, the American Jewish Committee and the National Community Relations Advisory Council. These organizations are geared to fight discrimination by legal means, by legislation, by public relations and by education. In addition they stimulate research into intergroup issues, support publications of many kinds, sponsor workshops on intergroup issues and conduct other kinds of intergroup programs and activities. The aim is to utilize established and publicly sanctioned procedures and agencies both for opposing discriminations and for expanding opportunities for the minorities. Typically, the Jews have maintained a concern for the well-being of all the minorities.

Traditionally, Jewish intellectuals and scholars have been active in liberal and pro-gressive organizations and movements. At all times also, Jews have been found in the ranks of the economic and political radicals. Their intellectual tradition as well as their interpretation of self-interest indicates that their chances for security and self-expression are optimal in social situations that are continuously and vitally democratic, free, and flexible. Thus this liberal-to-radical orientation of Jewish intellectual and philosophical life constitutes an aspect of the politcal posture of this minority group.

Historically, the Japanese and Chinese in the United States have tended to be withdrawn and conservative. Many of their organizations have been parochial in nature, concerned mainly with private matters of customs, religion, and business, or devoted to protection against the hostile whites. The traumatic wartime experience of the Japanese in the Relocation Centers seems to have made little impact on the political orientations of the Japanese. The Chinese have maintained their disengagement from American issues by limiting much of their activity and concerns to the confines of Chinatowns.

Yet, as suggested, some stirrings of protest can be observed within the Chinese communities. Some of the young Chinese, especially in San Francisco, New York, and Chicago, have espoused the posture of militancy and toyed with the tactics of violence. Middle-class Japanese and Chinese have tended to act alone in ways that facilitate their chances of assimilation into the surrounding dominant society. This pattern is

9. Milton M. Gordon, *Assimilation in American Life* (New York: Oxford, 1964), pp. 175-176. Marden and Meyer, *Minorities in American Society*, pp. 412, 415, and Simpson and Yinger, *Racial and Cultural Minorities*, pp. 413-414.

evidenced by joining Protestant churches, settling in middle-class neighborhoods and intermarriage with whites.

STRATEGIC STYLES

These accounts of inter-group conflict indicate that the racial and ethnic minorities are impatient to achieve full membership in the society. They can no longer rely on the good will of the dominants or the impersonal operation of the process of assimilation. Instead, they struggle for full societal membership in ways that have been called "politics."

The foregoing accounts of the minority efforts reveal three basic approaches to struggle which are called "strategic styles." They are "institutional integration," "secession," and "social assimilation." These strategic styles suggest that the minorities have made different assessments of their situation and prospects within American society. They also set crucial problems for the formulation and application of public policy.

Analytic models of the strategic styles can be constructed of the following four components:

1. A collective judgment of "legitimate rights" or the appropriate goals of endeavor.
2. An assessment of the nature, location, and strength of the obstacles to be overcome.
3. An assessment of the chances of achieving success, and therefore of the kind and amount of effort required to achieve success.
4. A choice, more or less explicit and rational, of the tactics required for this effort.

By means of this analytic model it is possible to differentiate the three strategic styles and classify the various minorities in terms of their political activities.

Institutional Integration

Institutional integration defines collective goals as the legitimate right to participate in all sectors and every rank of the society's bureaucratic apparatus.* Basic are the occupational roles of the economy and the power positions of the politico-governmental apparatus. Institutional integration also includes all the ranks of the other formal institutions, education, housing, the military, and religion, to mention the more obvious ones.

Two controversial situations can serve to illustrate the meaning of this goal. In education, institutional integration means total and absolute school desegregation of students and teachers even if that requires massive busing. In housing, it means open housing in the complete and basic sense of that phrase. What is claimed by the minorities is the right to participate in these quasi-public bureaucracies to the same degree and in the same manner as the dominants.

From the institutional integration perspective the minorities perceive the main obstacle as legal and quasi-legal rules of bureaucratic action. These are matters of public policy and customary relations. The opposition is focused in the power and structure of the society's bureaucratic apparatus and, therefore is very powerful.

Such an estimate of the nature, location and strength of the opposition suggests that, from this perspective, the minorities can-

*Cf. "Bureaucratic integration," Chapter 4.

not be sanguine about their chances of success within the forseeable future. It is a long, hard, up-hill struggle in which gains come gradually and grudgingly and in which there is no assurance of ultimate success.

As a consequence, such estimates and judgments argue for power wielding tactics. These range from the non-violence of marches and demonstrations to the violences of disturbances and riots, from the sentimentality of kneelings and children's marches to the instrumentality of power politics and consumer pressure. Sometimes explicitly, perhaps more often implicitly, group struggle reveals some calculation of tactical means to the requirements of collective ends.

Typically, the strategic objective of blacks, Mexicans, Puerto Ricans and perhaps Chinese is institutional integration. The political efforts of these minorities indicate an estimate of their situation and prospects, for which institutional integration seems to be the most appropriate approach. In every case, though, some individuals and sub-groups advocate one of the other styles. Some nationalist blacks, Puerto Ricans and Mexicans have opted for secession as the proper approach to struggle. Some Puerto Ricans and Chinese prefer to strive for social assimilation into the dominant society. However, for most members of these groups, the norm of color and culture limits the realistic possibility of social assimilation.

Secession

Secession as a strategic pattern refers to collective struggle for ecological separation and local political autonomy. The group perceives the society as opressive and estimates that it cannot achieve its legitimate aims within the oppressive societal system. The minority group must therefore withdraw into an ecological and political situation where it can maintain cultural and societal integrity and can manage its collective affairs. Both institutional integration and social assimilation are recognized as unattainable within the existing societal situation, and (if they were possible) unacceptable to the group that wishes to perpetuate its independent societal existence.

Secession has long been the conflict pattern of the American Indians. Sometimes it has been envisaged as territorial separation and full political independence. More often, though, it has meant the development within the national society of segregated homogeneous enclaves that enjoy self-determination. The central elements of the secession strategy of the Indians include the following:

1. Originally, and by sacred right, all the land of continental United States belonged to our ancestors.
2. Immorally and illegally, by force and by bribery, the whites took this land from our Indian forebears.
3. The land, therefore, rightfully still belongs to us, their descendants.
4. We demand that the white man's government compensate us for this land, and permit us to live unmolested on those parts of the territory that we shall select.
5. However, since we have found that the white man will not accede to these legitimate demands, we feel justified in resorting to any means of struggle that seem necessary to achieve our legitimate claim.

For a long time secession has also persisted as a minor conflict theme among blacks in the United States. At one time it was phrased as the "back to Africa movement;" later it took the form of the "Forty-Ninth State" plan; and more recently it has appeared as various formulations of black nationalism.

Social Assimilation

Social assimilation is the strategic approach of those minorities who face few and limited barriers to institutional integration. If the groups are also white, then the norm of color raises no insuperable obstacle to full inclusion in the life of the dominant sector. The democratic tradition favors social assimilation. Subcultural deviations may be muted and justified by the advocacy of pluralism. Moreover, striving for full inclusion in all aspects of the society is consonant with the thrust of the national ethos.

Under the aegis of social assimilation, the striving is for inclusion within the dominant society at the informal clique and intimate friendship levels. What is at stake is participation in clubs, cliques, parties and receptions, family exchange (e.g., dinner invitations), the courtship and marriage of children. The aspiring minority people must acquire the psycho-cultural lore of dominant white society. Moreover, they must come to think of themselves as members of that social sector and, in the end, be fully accepted as members.

It is partly metaphorical to refer to this collective effort as "struggle" or "politics," for the tactics employed are not the methods of conflict. Instead the striving group does those things that it calculates are likely to make it acceptable to the dominants. At the same time the group must be alert to the possibility of rebuffs and poised for defense against subtle discrimination.

The minority for which social assimilation would seem to be most feasible and appropriate is the Jews. Yet, as suggested, the dominants tend to block their admission to the level of informal and intimate participation. It is a matter of neither accident nor policy that middle- and upper-middle-class Jews maintain their own networks of clique relationships. It seems likely that these advantaged Jews would like to be accepted into dominant American society as they are for what they are. Meanwhile, being denied this goal, they make themselves acceptable and guard against subtle discriminations.

A small, select group of Puerto Ricans, Japanese, and Chinese find that they can practice the strategy of social assimilation. These are persons of high education, prestigious occupational rank, and advanced assimilation to the dominant patterns. The "fortunate" Puerto Ricans are likely to be mainland-born mulattoes who can "pass." Often these persons signal their success in social assimilation by marrying members of the dominant group.

By the very nature of the case, the groups and individuals who espouse the strategy of social assimilation tend to be conservative in intergroup politics. They cannot, or at least they believe they cannot, afford to rock the boat they are trying so hard to enter. The politics of militancy is reserved for those minority members who by virtue of color and/or culture have no hope of entering the dominant group.

AN EXPLANATION OF MINORITY-GROUP CONFLICT

At this time the student may ask why the American dream of assimilation failed and why the minorities have drifted toward militant conflict. The answer to this question can serve two useful ends. First, if conditions continue as they now are, it can help him to see what may happen in minority-dominant relations in the foreseeable future. And second, this answer may provide a basis for discussing policies and programs in the field of intergroup relations. This topic is taken up in the next chapter.

From the very beginning, relations between the minorities and the dominants were always a mixture of antagonism and comradeship, of conflict and cooperation. The national system, however, was organized in such a way as to guarantee that the antagonisms and conflicts remained within tolerable limits. This end was achieved in part by keeping the minorities in inferior and segregated positions, relatively powerless and unorganized. Moreover, each side, minorities and dominants, needed the other and so cooperation was necessary for survival and well-being.

However, the national system was not only dominating and controlling; it was also unstable and changing. In the nineteenth and twentieth centuries, the United States experienced a series of dramatic changes that fundamentally altered the situation of the minorities in the national society. Among other changes these included a series of wars, conquest of the frontier, the American Industrial Revolution, unification of the nation and abolition of slavery in the Civil War, massive European immigration and the growth of great cities, the establishment of public education, and a great multi-faceted humanitarian movement. In these events and processes of change, the ranks, functions and powers of the minority groups were modified. One consequence of these developments was modification of the cooperation-conflict dichotomy that had characterized relations between minorities and dominants.

The potential for aggressive, overt struggle by the minorities was built into the unstable changing system.[10] The tradition of the society stressed democracy, equality and achievement. Acculturation and Americanization transmitted these values and goals to the minority peoples. The more they assimilated American culture, the more irksome they found their minority-group status and limitations. On the one hand, the national system urged the minority peoples forward to assimilation and through assimilation to full participation in the society; on the other hand, it held them back by institutionalized barriers of segregation and discrimination.

Within the unstable national system the potential for aggressive struggle by the minorities was actualized during the decades of the 1950s and 1960s. Five social factors operating in a cluster were decisive in producing this shift in the amount and intensity of minority-group conflict. The five factors are:

1. Heightened motivation to increased collective struggle for full rights and participation.
2. Organization for carrying out collective struggle.
3. Acquisition of the power resources needed to prosecute the struggle.
4. Borrowing or development of appropriate conflict tactics.

10. See I. and R. Feierabend and Betty Nesvold, "Social Change and Political Violence; Cross-National Patterns," in eds., Hugh D. Graham and Ted Gurr, *The History of Violence in America* (New York: Praeger, 1969) pp. 632-687.

5. The occurrence of adequate catalyzing or triggeriing events.

The capacity of these factors to cause collective conflict rests in the fact and manner of their linkage and reenforcement. Each factor is added in the order shown in the list and linked in operation with the preceding ones. This addition and linkage of factors increased the possibility of overt aggressive conflict while reducing the chances that conflict would either remain constant or decline. In the end, this process ensured that the increase of conflict by the minorities was the only outcome that could occur.

Summary

The history of each of the minorities in the twentieth century reveals their disappointment with moderation and assimilation as the method of reducing segregation and discrimination. This disappointment was followed by recourse to more direct and militant methods that were called the politics of minority status. The analysis indicated that all these collective struggles can be classified in three major strategic styles called institutional integration, secession, and social assimilation. The first style seemed to fit the blacks, Mexicans, Puerto Ricans, and some Chinese. The Indians were seen as secessionist, and social assimilation appeared to be most feasible for the Jews and some Japanese, Puerto Ricans, and Chinese. The chapter concluded with a brief hypothetical model that offered an explanation of the upsurge of struggle and militancy among the minority groups.

For Further Reading

Bennett, Lerone. *Confrontation Black and White,* Baltimore: Penguin, 1965.

This is a descriptive analysis of the black revolt in America.

Brown, Dee. *Bury My Heart at Wounded Knee,* New York: Bantam Books, 1972.

A history of the plunder of the American Indians in the second half of the last century.

Conot, Robert. *Rivers of Blood, Years of Darkness,* New York: Morrow, 1968.

A full historical account of the Watts Riot of 1965.

Eddy, Elizabeth M. *Walk the White Line: A Profile of Urban Education,* Garden City: Doubleday Anchor, 1967.

This book asks whether white middle-class education can succeed in inner city racial and ethnic minorities.

Grier, William H. and Cobbs, Price M. *Black Rage,* Basic Books, 1969.

Two psychiatrists examine the anger of blacks that preceeded the riots of the 1960's.

Himes, Joseph S. *Racial Conflict in American Society,* Columbus (OH): Merrill, 1973.

A sociological study of conflict by blacks in the 1960s and 1970s.

Josephy, Alvin M. Jr., "Wounded Knee and All That: What the Indians Want," *New York Times Magazine* March 18, 1973, pp. 18ff.

A frank examination of Indian conflict by a competent Indian scholar.

Waskow, Arthur I. *From Race Riot to Sit-In: 1919 and the 1960s,* Garden City: Doubleday Anchor, 1966.

Summary comparison of racial crises of 1919 and the 1960's, both times of great riots.

6 | Policy and Action in Intergroup Relations

SINCE 1850, the United States has been the most racially and ethnically mixed collection of people in the world. They came, some fifty million of them, by migration from every continent, mainly Europe. Other millions were acquired by conquest, colonialism and annexation. Some of them intermarried and exchanged their cultures, thus adding new tones of diversity to the mixture.

From the beginning the diversity of races and cultures was seen as a problem. George Washington, John Adams and Thomas Jefferson deplored the deviation of the newcomers from the English standard they had established.[1] Throughout the nineteenth century the dominants reacted to the growing diversity in a series of "nativist" movements and actions.[2] As the tide of immigration swelled in the last quarter of the nineteeth and first quarter of the twentieth centuries, opposition to diversity increased. It climaxed in passage of the immigration restriction laws between 1921 and 1927.

As amalgamation in the melting pot and Anglo-American assimilation failed, intergroup hostility and conflict increased. The minorities demanded and won the right to cultural integrity in the ideology of "cul-

tural pluralism." Following the Second World War the pressure for social justice and material improvement took a more direct and aggressive form.

By the 1960s the former problem of racial and cultural diversity had become the problem of minority-group conflict. Its most dramatic expressions were riots in the 1960s and insurrection in the 1970s. Reflecting on the riots of 1964 to 1967, the National Advisory Commission on Civil Disorders declared:

Our nation is moving toward two societies, one black, one white—separate and unequal. Reaction to ... disorders [1964 to 1967] has quickened the movement and deepened the division. Discrimination and segregation have long per-

1. See the opinions quoted by Milton M. Gordon, *Assimilation in American Life* (New York: Oxford, 1964), pp. 89-94. Roy L. Garis, *Immigration* (New York:Macmillan, 1972), Chapters 1 and 2. Maurice R. Davie, *World Immigration* (New York: Macmillan, 1936), Chapter 2. W. C. Ford, ed., *The Writings of George Washington* (New York: Putnam, 1889), Vol. 12, p. 489. Saul K. Pacover, ed., *Notes on Virginia: Thomas Jefferson on Democracy* (New York: New American Library, 1945), query 8.

2. See John Higham, *Strangers in the Land* (New Brunswick, N.J.: Rutgers University Press, 1955), Chapter 1.

meated much of American life; they now threaten the future of every American.

Segregation poverty have created in the racial ghetto a destructive environment totally unknown to most white Americans. What white Americans have never fully understood—but what the Negro can never forget—is that white society is deeply implicated in the ghetto. White institutions created it, white institutions maintain it, and white society condones it.

To pursue our present course will involve the continuing polarization of the American community and, ultimately, the destruction of basic democratic values.[3]

Yet, despite the extravagant diversity of types and the periodic crises, the United States has never achieved a consistent policy and action orientation for dominant-minority relations. Instead, a variety of ideologies, traditions, and proposals have arisen to influence this sphere of social relations. One consequence of this situation has been national disunity, social drift, and periodic crisis. For example, in March, 1973, the urgent need for a clear policy and definitive program was dramatized by paramilitary occupation and confrontation at Wounded Knee, South Dakota, by a band of Indians under the auspicies of The American Indian Movement in what some officials have called "insurrection."[4]

THE TRADITION OF CONFORMITY

From the beginning, the dominant and growing Anglo-American group expected, almost naturally it seemed, that newcomers would be like them. This expectation did not express a formal decision or collective action. Nevertheless, the dominants viewed this expectation as a rule, binding on themselves and the newcomers alike, and sanctioned by their superior authority. This in-

formal judgment about what should happen to outsiders has persisted through every period of national history and constitutes a kind of baseline of social policy for dominant-minority relations.

Assimilation

Public officials, social scientists, and writers have formalized the expectations of the dominants in the concept of assimilation. In its most basic form, assimilation meant learned conformity to the values and norms of the Anglo-American complex. Such a policy was necessitated by the norm of color and culture that was established early in the history of the society. People must be like the dominants in socially and politically significant ways, or they must be excluded from the major rights and opportunities of the society. To be like the dominants, the newcomers had to be white, and both able and willing to master the Anglo-American culture system. Immigrants from the United Kingdom and from Northwest Europe, especially Scandinavia, the Netherlands, and Germany, seemed most suitable for assimilation.

Until the end of the nineteenth century, the process of assimilation tended to be rather casual and voluntary. The newcomers were invited to conform, and rewarded by acceptance into the dominant group. The leaders of the colonies and states discouraged the formation of enclaves of immigrants with alien ways. For example,

3. National Advisory Commission on Civil Disorders, *Report* (New York: Bantam Books, 1968), pp. 1-2.
4. See Alvin M. Josephy, Jr., "Wounded Knee and All That—What the Indians Want," *New York Times Magazine*, (March 18, 1973) pp. 18 ff.

Benjamin Franklin persuaded the Germans not to multiply ethnic communities in Pennsylvania.[5]

The first serious challenge to this informal method of assimilation came in 1849 and 1850 with large-scale immigration of famine-fleeing Irish peasants and poor Germans.[6] These newcomers not only differed significantly from the old Anglo-American stock; they also tended to settle in ethnic enclaves both in big Eastern cities and in the rural West. The Civil War disrupted the easy-going pattern of life and assimilation that had grown up.

Americanization

After the Civil War when the volume of immigration increased sharply, and when the immigrants began to come from Southeast Europe, it became evident that voluntary assimilation was inadequate. To meet this changed situation so-called "Americanization" programs were initiated. Alien ways were disparaged and the immigrants were pressured, often virtually forced, to learn and glorify American values and institutions. Many lineage-patriotic organizations like the D.A.R. and the S.A.R., business and industrial firms, and governmental units, especially in big eastern cities, advocated and supported these Americanization activities.[7] This method of enforced assimilation reached its peak during the First World War and thereafter quickly declined. In the early 1920s Americanization was replaced by legislation to restrict the volume, and to control the type of immigration.

Amalgamation

The rising tide of "new" immigration also supported renewed interest in the melting pot idea. However, even though this approach to the problems of the newcomers had some eloquent advocates, it never really got beyond the stage of rhetoric and advocacy. Amalgamation implied intermarriage as the main step of assimilation, whereas the basic ideology of Anglo-American conformity envisaged intermarriage as the terminal phase of the process. As it turned out in fact, Anglo-American assimilation is typically not fully accomplished before the second or third generation.

Deviations from the Norm

Cultural pluralism and the situation of the non-white minorities constitute deviations from the pattern of assimilation envisaged by the norm of color and culture. Seeing the new breed of newcomers as virtually unassimilable and unamalgamable, many people became reconciled to leaving them undisturbed in their ethnic enclaves, provided of course they did not become a public problem. The confession of failure of assimilation was legitimized by calling it "cultural pluralism." Anglo-American conformity was reduced to an informal and voluntary process. At the instance of official leaders, social scientists, and popular writers, cultural pluralism was developed into an important intergroup ideology which many saw as the policy route to the future in this field.

From the beginning, assimilation was never offered to the non-white minorities. They were unacceptable because they could never meet the dominants' standard

5. Garis, *Immigration Restriction*, Chapters 1 and 2.
6. Higham, *Strangers in the Land*, Chapter 1.
7. See Chapter 4 of this book.

of color. Once taken this decision had two lasting consequences for American society. First, it necessitated a caste-type position in the social structure as a permanent place for the non-white minorities. And second, it insured that the principle permanent minorities would be racial, since in time most of the whites could expect to be absorbed into the dominant group.

THE CIVIL RIGHTS APPROACH

When the United States Constitution was written and when the government was established, it was generally believed that "social relations" was not a proper area of official action. To meet the need for control and order in relations between the dominant and growing minority groups, the norm of color and culture was fashioned. In the two centuries that elapsed since the founding of the nation, the government has assumed more and more responsibility for ordering social relations. At the present time, therefore, the federal government, and indeed also the several state and local governments take many actions that affect policy in the field of dominant-minority relations.

Since the management of social relations was not considered a proper responsibility of government, no provisions were written into the Constitution authorizing the Congress and President to act in this field. However, in the intervening years students of the Constitution have found several "clauses" that either authorize or permit the Congress to act. The most noteworthy are the "general welfare," the "interstate commerce" and the "equal protection of the law" provisions.

Because of this circumstance in the framing of the Constitution, the federal govern-

ment has not taken the initiative in controlling social relations. Rather, it has reacted to problems by taking legislative action. For example, it was only *after* the Constitution had been ratified and the government established that it was discovered that no protection of individual rights had been written. In response to this situation the Bill of Rights was added to the Constitution. The inclusive Civil Rights Act of 1964 was the government's reply to the years of agitation and struggle by the minority groups. Every day the courts react to intergroup problems and formulate decisions, some of which become important precedents. However, even though the federal government reacts to intergroup problems, its amendments, laws and decisions are an important source of policy in this field.

The following four types of federal governmental pronouncements serve to establish policy and guide action in intergroup relations:

1. Amendments to the Constitution.
2. Enactments by the Congress.
3. Decisions of the courts interpreting laws within the framework of the Constitution.
4. Orders and regulations issued by executive and administrative units that interpret the laws for purposes of their administration.

The federal government was late getting into the business of making intergroup policy. Its progress in this field can be sketched by reference to amendments to the Constitution. Legislation, administrative orders, and court decisions tend to follow and elaborate the provisions written into the Constitution. The first major step was ratification of the Bill of Rights in 1791. This package of ten amendments stipulated the basic rights of the individual that were considered to be inherent in his role as citizen and member of the society. The second major civil rights step was the adoption of the so-called Civil War amendments, numbers 13, 14, and 15. While these actions abolished the institution of slavery and incorporated the freed blacks into the political society, they also enhanced the basic rights of all citizens. A series of amendments granted the franchise (and a cluster of correlated rights) progressively to poor people, blacks, women, and most recently young persons. Each of these series of amendments required, encouraged, or permitted legislation, administrative orders, and court decisions that translated their special provisions into the fabric of normative intergroup relations.

Policy Aspects of Civil Rights Enactments

By implication these legal actions of the federal government made policy in the area of dominant-minority relations. The government was dealing with relatively specific public issues. Often, however, these enactments inaugurated new policy because they were extended and generalized to cover many other related or analogous situations. At least three specific ways can be identified in which these legislative and legal steps influence social policy and action in the field of intergroup relations.

First, all civil rights legislation and actions focus on the relations between the highstationed and the inferior, the powerful and the powerless, and the accepted and the rejected in the society. That is, the thrust of civil rights enactments is the relationship nexus between the dominants and minorities. This is true because (as shown in Chapter 1) the dominants control the higher statuses and major power in the society.

This policy implication of civil rights enactments can be illustrated in the spheres that have been recently under consideration. The Voting Rights Act of 1965 prohibited the political dominants from interfering with minority peoples in exercising the right to register and vote. This relationship nexus is most significant in the case of blacks in many southern areas. School desegregation decisions and acts alter relations between whites and blacks in the same way. A restraint is laid upon the dominant group, and the action possibilities of the minority are thereby enhanced.

Second, civil rights actions establish and sanction new norms of intergroup relations. In selected areas (e.g., travel, and public accommodations) the civil rights action abrogates the pattern of segregation and discrimination required by the traditional norm for this relationship. Further, this action brings the sanction of governmental power to the support of the new intergroup norm.

Through civil-rights action, the norms governing relations with Mexicans in the Southwest are under constant modification. Most of these developments have concerned the protection and rights of migratory and seasonal farm workers. In the same way the patterns of relations with the Indians have been undergoing change. In 1970, President Nixon sought to institute "self-determination" as the norm in relations with the numerous Indian "nations" and "tribes." However, failure of Congress to pass the necessary enabling legislation tended to impede this change.[8]

8. Josephy, "Wounded Knee and All That That," pp. 18 ff.

Third, and crucially, the civil rights approach to intergroup policy transforms the new intergroup norms, for example desegregation, voting rights, or self-determination, into inherent dimensions of the citizen role. Thus the action is changed from an unofficial interpersonal relationship to an official right of citizens. Such a transfer is crucial, for as citizens ,dominants, and minority people are statutory equals. To put the matter another way, the relationship is shifted from a particularistic to a universalistic normative pattern. This shift is a crucial aspect of the policy implications of governmental civil rights action.

In sum, civil rights action by the government functions to influence intergroup policy in several ways. Such actions modify and rearrange relations between the dominants and minorities. They also tend to erode the coverage, power, and legitimacy of the traditional norm of color and culture. They establish and sanction new norms in the arena of intergroup relations. And finally, government action operates to transfer relationships from the particularistic arena of informal, unofficial action to the universalistic sphere of citizen rights.

Other Government Actions

It can be argued that in the civil rights arena, intergroup policy has developed rather consistently. This cannot be said for actions of the government in other spheres. In many ways the government has either enacted or sanctioned the norm of color and culture, thus tending to limit or circumvent requirements of its civil rights standards.

Slavery was abolished as a by-product of the Civil War.[9] Many official actions of the Executive, the Congress, and the courts aided resubjugation and control of the blacks. Noteworthy were abolition of the Freedman's Bureau, passage of the so-called "black codes," and Supreme Court decisions like Plessy vs. Ferguson. Thus, in spite of the civil-rights positions of the Bill of Rights, the Civil War Amendments, and other actions, the government either disregarded the Bill of Rights, or supported and sanctioned reinstatement of the traditional norm of color and culture. By the end of the nineteenth century it was evident that this traditional norm was "the policy" for relations between whites and blacks.

The United States has acquired a reputation for colonial relations with non-white peoples. The Philippine Islands were taken from Spain and held in colonial status until being granted independence in 1946. Hawaii and Alaska were administered as "territories" until admitted to statehood in 1959. Puerto Rico and the Virgin Islands remain as United States "territories." In the 1960s and on into the 1970's the United States has experienced stormy relations with the Republic of Panama over the ownership and administration of the Panama Canal Zone.

One of the most depressing records in national history is that of the dominants' relations with the indigenous Indian population.[10] From the beginning they were treated with indifference, contempt, and hostility. In time they were decimated and confined within reservations. For more than a century the government has struggled with the issue of a "policy" for the Indians. Always, however, this issue is beclouded by

9. See John Hope Franklin, *From Slavery to Freedom* (New York: Vintage, 1969), Chapter 16.
10. Josephy, "Wounded Knee and All That," pp. 18 ff.

judgments and strictures of the traditional norm of color and culture.

Equally reprehensible was treatment of the Japanese on the West Coast during the Second World War. Following the attack on Pearl Harbor on December 7, 1941, the Japanese, foreign-born immigrants and their native-born citizen children alike, were suspected of potential treason. Tormented by a sense of urgency and menace, the government made the decision to remove the entire Japanese population from the "vulnerable" West Coast. With great personal sacrifice and loss they were transported and confined in so-called Relocation Centers in the interior.[11]

In times of crisis the society, and representing it, the government, often tends to observe a moratorium with respect to its civil rights positions. One of these civil rights moratoria was the passage of restrictive immigration legislation following the First World War. The so-called "quota" formula was devised and arranged so as to limit immigration from Asia and Southeast Europe, areas from which recent immigrants had come.

POLICY AND ACTION PROPOSALS

In the face of their experiences with assimilation, denial of civil rights, colonialism and governmental abuses, there can be little wonder that the racial and ethnic minorities are dissatisfied with the present situation. Their discontents are expressed in the conflict strategies and enterprises that were reviewed in the previous chapter. Implicit in these manifestations of the "politics of minority status" are social policies ranging from the striving for social assimilation to the espousal of revolution and secession.

Criticism of the minority-group status and advocacy of alternative policy-action programs have also been taken up by public leaders and social scientists, themselves not directly involved in the minority-group struggles.[12] Some of these proposals have been translated, in part at least, into public policy and programs, for example, the civil rights and anti-poverty programs and agencies of the Lyndon Johnson Administration. Many other proposals continue as part of the "great debate" around this issue. The concluding section of this book is addressed to the question of what should be our policy and action approach in the area of dominant-minority relations. But first we will review briefly several proposals to indicate the range of types and to present the main ideas that are woven together in the last part of the chapter to formulate a balanced proposal.

Some Policy Action Proposals

In the course of dealing with the issue of minorities in American society, many serious and imaginative ideas have been offered by concerned people. Some have argued that the minority groups must help themselves, accelerating conformity to the Anglo-American model and thus making themselves acceptable to the dominant white group.[13] We have seen that voluntary

11. See Leonard Blum and Ruth Riemer, *Removal and Return* (Berkeley: University of California Press, 1949); and Alexander H. Leighton, *The Governing of Men* (Princeton: Princeton University Press, 1945).

12. In this connection see Hubert H. Humphrey, *Beyond Civil Rights* (New York: Random House, 1968).

13. See George E. Simpson and J. Milton Yinger, *Racial and Cultural Minorities* (New York: Harper and Row, 1972), Chapters 21 and 22.

assimilation through cultural conformity has proved to be impossible for most of the current racial and ethnic minorities. The term "nationalism" is used to designate those policies and programs that seek adjustment through withdrawal and limited control within residential enclaves. This approach is most characteristic of some Indian groups and a few black organizations.[14] A few extremist individuals and organizations in several of the minorities have advocated societal reconstruction in a way that totally and permanently eliminates prejudicial and discriminatory values and practices.[15] In this discussion we will sketch three proposals: cultural pluralism, cultural pluralism combined with governmental action, and massive societal reform.

Cultural pluralism designates one of the most persuasive approaches to the issue of the nation's racial and ethnic groups. Many, perhaps most thoughtful people now advocate, or at least agree to group autonomy and non-conformity at the *communal*, i.e., subcultural and primary-group level. Implicitly, and occasionally explicitly also, cultural pluralism is included in a proposal in this field.

The ideology of pluralism begins with recognition that the racial and ethnic minorities tend to resist giving up their traditional culture and organization at the communal level. Autonomy and diversity at this private level are judged to be consistent with democratic values, provided the minority groups conform at the public level of institutional life and action. The individual's identity is confirmed at the group level— black, Mexican, or Indian; the societal level —American; and the global level— human being.[16] This combination of diversity is said to produce richness, unity, and strength in the general society.

Charles F. Marden and Gladys Meyer have provided a statement of the cultural pluralism policy position.[17] By implication they seem to recognize that under the Christian democratic ethic, the only consistent solution to the problem of the racial and ethnic minorities is assimilation via the melting pot route. However, they also perceive that this solution is not feasible in American society as presently constituted. In the face of this dilemma they see cultural pluralism as operating in two ways to provide an escape and solution. For the white descendents of European immigrants who are assimilable, cultural pluralism constitutes a half-way station on the way to ultimate disappearance into the growing and changing dominant group. For the non-white minorities, for whom ultimate assimilation seems doubtful, and for those whites who elect not to assimilate, they see the stabilized cultural pluralistic society as the ideal ultimate solution.

Writing in 1963 against the background of the black non-violence civil rights protest movement, Milton M. Gordon outlined a policy-action model based on three principles.[18] First, he argued that subcultural pluralism and primary group integrity would characterize the situation of the mi-

14. E. U. Essien-Udom, *Black Nationalism* (Chicago: University of Chicago Press, 1962); and Josephy, "Wounded Knee and All That," pp. 18 ff.

15. This approach has been advocated by such groups as the Black Panthers and The Young Lords for Puerto Ricans.

16. Milton M. Gordon, *Assimilation in American Life* (New York: Oxford, 1964), p. 265.

17. Charles F. Marden and Gladys Meyer, *Minorities in American Society* (New York: American Book Company, 1968), p. 51.

18. Gordon, *Assimilation*, Chapter 8.

norities for the foreseeable future. He believed that both patterns were consistent with democratic values and might have only limited effect upon group prejudice. Second, he felt strongly that the minorities themselves had at least two responsibilities in this matter. They should present the facts of their lives, both favorable and unfavorable. The minorities should be responsible for guiding their members toward conformity, and curbing antisocial and deviant conduct of their members. He believed that such actions would win confidence and favor among the dominants. And third, Gordon declared that the goverment had responsibility to enforce desegregation of the major institutions and areas of public life. The minorities would continue their organized struggles to press the government forward to this task and to effect continuing reduction of group prejudice and modification of sub-legal discrimination.

The National Advisory Commission on Civil Disorders in its 1968 *Report* sketched an imperious, massive, and crash program for solving the problems of the black minority. The items of this program contain the elements of a policy-action model for dominant-minority relations.

It is time to adopt strategies for action that will produce quick and visible progress. Our recommendations embrace three basic principles: (1) To mount programs on a scale equal to the dimension of the problems; (2) To aim these programs for high impact in the immediate future in order to close the gap between promise and performance; (3) To undertake new initiatives and experiments that can change the system of failure and frustration that now dominates the ghetto and weakens our society. These programs will require unprecedented levels of funding and performance .... There can be no higher priority for national action and no higher claim on the nation's conscience.[19]

A Proposal

A policy for dominant-minority relations can be fashioned of the ideas presented in the foregoing paragraphs. Such a proposal is sketched in the accompanying tabulation and is seen to contain three major components: goals, a role for the government, and responsibilities of the groups themselves.

COMPONENTS OF AN INTERGROUP POLICY

I. Goals

    A. Mandatory institutional change enabling full bureaucratic assimilation of the minorities.

    B. Sanctioned right of all groups (dominant as well as minorities) to communal, i.e., individual sub-cultural and primary-group autonomy.

II. Action: Role of Government

    A. Marshall and mobilize the resources required to achieve these goals.

    B. Enforce the change required to enable bureaucratic assimilation of the minorities.

    C. Facilitate harmonious intergroup relations by means of human relations agencies, programs and the like.

III. Action: Role of the Groups

    A. Support and thus validate the goals and responsibility of government.

    B. Actions to facilitate and advance the general goals.

19. National Advisory Commission on Civil Disorders, *Report* pp. 1-2.

The national experience with assimilation, Americanization, and the melting pot have made it clear that total absorption of the racial and ethnic minorities into the dominant group is neither possible nor necessary. As shown in the list, a policy of intergroup relations should reflect this fact. The policy outline therefore specifies that "bureaucratic assimilation" should be mandatory, but group autonomy should be retained at the level of subcultural and primary-group affairs. In the case of the Indians living on reservations, this right would include political "self-determination" analogous to that now exercised by the fifty states. Such a policy proposal combines assimilation at the societal level with pluralism at the communal level. This proposal conforms to the realities of social life in the United States and seems likely to minimize intergroup frictions. Moreover, such an arrangement is fully consistent with democratic values.

National experience has also shown that all the minorities are not equally integrated into all roles and ranks of the bureaucratic institutions and organizations. Segregation and discrimination, prescribed by the norm of color and culture, excludes some minority individuals from positions in all areas. It will therefore be necessary for the government to enforce "desegregation" and "nondiscrimination" as a precondition to assimilation at this level. It should be a responsibility of government to marshall and mobilize whatever resources of wealth and power may be needed to carry out this program.

Once these opportunities are open to the minority people, recruitment and participation can be managed by traditional democratic principles of merit and competition.

The National Commission of Civil Disorders has indicated that massive resources may be required in another way. They must be invested in readying minority people for these opportunities and in offsetting the disadvantages resulting from generations of segregation and discrimination. Use of public authority and resources for this purpose is a legitimate activity of government within the democratic tradition.

Government should act to facilitate harmonious relations among the various groups in the realms of intergroup association that may be impeded by communal autonomy. The human relations approach is an established strategy for this task. The aim is twofold, both to resolve limited disputes and to advance understanding and rewarding contacts on the personal and small-group level. The human relations technique can serve to harmonize the personal relations that are improved by the desegregation of the bureaucracies.

And finally, the groups themselves, dominant as well as minorities, have a crucial responsibility under such a policy. They must accept the goals and responsibilities of government in this area. In this way they can validate the policy and support the functions of the government. In addition, as suggested, the dominants must accept the goals and means of such a policy and seek to bring it into realization. The dominants and minorities alike must search for the truth in their relationships and seek to adjust their behavior to such facts.

The structural framework envisaged by such a policy might establish a way for the minorities to live in the society in relative security and harmony. It is less than the

20. *Ibid.*, p. 1.

ideal implied by the ethic of political democracy and Christianity. However, it represents substantial and significant advance over the present intergroup situation. To achieve even this less than ideal solution will require vast investments of resources and dedication. Yet, as the National Advisory Commission on Civil Disorders declared in 1968, time is running out and the options are limited. One can only hope the nation will get on with this business with all deliberate speed.[20]

Summary

From the beginning national leaders saw racial and ethnic diversity as a problem. They discouraged fragmentation of the society by establishment of nationality communities. Yet a consistent policy for managing these relations was never formulated.

The reaction to this problem has been expressed in several ways. Traditionally, it was assumed that all newcomers would become American through assimilation. Later, the government acted reluctantly to deal with the problem through the civil rights approach. Throughout though, the government and other institutions have supported the norm of color and culture in managing dominant-minority relations.

In recent years thoughtful people have brought forward a series of policy proposals for dealing with this issue. This chapter ends with a proposal combining the most viable present ideas and an earnest wish for speedy action in the matter.

For Further Reading

Brotz, Howard M. *The Black Jews of Harlem,* New York: Schocken Books, 1970.

An examination of black leaders and the strategy of black nationalism in the American Scene.

Burger, Morroe. *Equality by Statute: The Revolution in Civil Rights,* Garden City: Doubleday Anchor, 1967.

Consideration of what law can and cannot do in the area of civil rights.

Deloria, Vine. *Of Utmost Good Faith,* New York: Bantam Books. 1972.

Precedent-setting judicial rulings, historical treaties, agreements and Congressional hearings tracing the development and change of national policy for the Indians.

Gordon, Milton M. *Assimilation in American Life,* New York: Oxford, 1964, Chapter 8.

Gordon presents his judgment of an appropriate intergroup policy.

Josephy, Alvin M. Jr., "Wounded Knee and All That," *New York Times Magazine,* March 18. 1973, pp. 18 ff.

A clear sketch of current government policy and inconsistency toward the Indians.

Marden, Charles F. and Meyer, Gladys. *Minorities in American Society,* New York: American Book Company, 1968, Part 3.

States the leading elements of intergroup policy as seen by these longtime students of minority relations.

Simpson, George E. and Yinger, J. Milton. *Racial and Cultural Minorities,* New York: Harper and Row, 1972, Part 3.

Sets out some policy requirements in intergroup relations, devoting attention to the role of cultural conformity by the minority people.

Glossary

Accommodation—The process of achieving and/or the structure of adjustment among groups, that tends to stress co-operation and reduce conflict.

Acculturation—The process of cultural change, and/or resultant cultural state, issuing from more or less continuous contact between groups with different cultures, in which one group gains or reformulates elements from the culture of the other group.

Alienation—A sense of detachment from society and loss of personal identity associated with social change, instability, and disorganization.

Amalgamation—The process of biological mixing, through marriage and extra-marital relations, in which different "races" or "stocks" are fused into a new stock. It always has cultural side effects.

Assimilation—(1) The process by which culturally different groups subordinate differences, expand similarities, and become fused in a new group. (2) The process in which one set of cultural traits is relinquished and a new set acquired. (3) The process by which a minority becomes incorporated into the system of social relations which constitutes the greater society.

Communal—The character of family and community life that results from informal social relations, kinship organization, traditional culture, and non-technical activities.

Conflict—Conflict, or social conflict, is struggle over scarce status, power, and resources, in which one group seeks to neutralize, injure, or eliminate the other.

Desegregation—Process of eliminating and/or the state of elimination of racial or ethnic segregation in public and quasi-public institutions and facilities.

Discrimination—The practice of distributing scarce values and opportunities unequally on the basis of unimportant or irrelevant racial and ethnic characteristics.

Ethnic—Refers to original national culture, religion, and race as distinguishing characteristics of a subgroup within an inclusive national group.

Ideology—A system of thought and belief that explains the past, interprets the present, predicts the future, and justifies present action.

59

Integration—(1) Process of achieving and/ or the resultant condition of more or less harmonious adjustment and relations among the parts of a social or cultural system. (2) State of relatively harmonious adjustment and relations between minorities and dominants. (3) Sometimes used to mean desegregation. See above.

Norm— Social or cultural norm, a pattern of social activity; socially required activity; generally expected activity; usual or customary activity.

Pluralism—(1) Cultural or societal, a peaceful coexistence of different groups. (2) A societal arrangement composed of a multiplicity of autonomous but interdependent groups. (3) A societal arrangement composed of a dominant group surrounded by a series of relatively autonomous and interdependent minority groups.

Prejudice—An emotional, rigid attitude toward a group of people. Similar to stereotype, see below.

Racial—Refers to physical characteristics, presumed to be hereditary, as the distinguishing features of a subgroup within an inclusive national group.

Secession—The act of withdrawing, either totally or partially, from a political state and of becoming more or less politically independent.

Segregation— Process of separating or state of separation of racial and ethnic minorities from the dominants, either geographically or in public or quasi-public institutions, because of physical and/or cultural criteria.

Social Policy—More or less rational agreements and decisions of a group regarding the ends and means of collective effort.

Social Structure—The more or less stable framework of social organization or of a social system.

Social System—The complex pattern of interrelations and operation of a set of parts that compose any unit of social organization.

Stereotype—A more or less standardized image of a group based in part on observed and in part on imagined characteristics, and serving to describe all members of the group, to predict their behavior and to prescribe how one should respond.

Subculture—A variant of an inclusive national culture that identifies the group that practices it as both a part of the inclusive society and different from the dominant group.

Index